WITH THE
"DIE-HARDS"
IN SIBERIA

COLONEL JOHN WARD
C.B., C.M.G., M.P.

The Naval & Military Press Ltd

❖

Reproduced by kind permission of the Central Library,
Royal Military Academy, Sandhurst

Published by

The Naval & Military Press Ltd

Unit 10, Ridgewood Industrial Park,

Uckfield, East Sussex,

TN22 5QE England

Tel: +44 (0) 1825 749494

Fax: +44 (0) 1825 765701

www.naval-military-press.com

© The Naval & Military Press Ltd 2004

COLONEL WARD, C.B., C.M.G., M.P.

To

MY COMRADES

OFFICERS, N.C.O.s AND MEN OF THE
18th, 19th, 25th AND 26th BATTALIONS OF
THE MIDDLESEX REGIMENT

who, on sea and land, in sunshine and snow, so
worthily upheld the traditional gallantry and
honour of their people and country

FOREWORD

ORIGINALLY written for the private use of my sons in case I did not return, this narrative of events connected with the expedition to Siberia must of necessity lack many of the necessary elements which go to make a history. I wrote of things as they occurred, and recorded the reasons and motives which prompted the participants. Many things have happened since which seem to show that we were not always right in our estimate of the forces at work around us. Things are not always what they seem, and this is probably more evident in the domain of Russian affairs than in any other. It would have been comparatively easy to alter the text and square it with the results, but that would have destroyed the main value of the story.

The statesman and the soldier rarely write history; it is their misfortune to make it. It is quite easy to be a prophet when you know the result. You can, as a rule, judge what a certain set of people will do in a certain set of circumstances, but where you deal with State policy which may be influenced by events and circumstances which have not the remotest connection with the question involved, it is impossible to give any forecast of their conduct on even the most elementary subject.

Foreword

The recent tragic events played out in the vast domain of Siberia are a case in point. It is certain that Admiral Koltchak would never have gone to Siberia, nor have become the head of the constitutional movement and government of Russia, if he had not been advised and even urged to do so by the Allies. He received the most categorical promises of whole-hearted support and early Allied recognition before he agreed to take up the dangerous duty of head of the Omsk Government. Had these urgings and promises been ungrudgingly performed a Constituent Assembly would be now sitting at Moscow hammering out the details of a Federal Constitution for a mighty Russian Republic or a parliamentary system similar to our own.

On the declaration of the Koltchak Government, General Denikin, General Dutoff, General Hovart, and the North Russian Governments made over their authority to Omsk. There was at once a clear issue —the Terrorist at Moscow, the Constitutionalist at Omsk. Had the Allies at this juncture translated their promises into acts, from what untold suffering Russia and Europe might have been saved!

The mere act of recognition would have created a wonderful impression on the Russian mind, in addition to giving the Allies a lever by which they could have guided the course of events and stabilised the Baltic. It would have given security to Russian finance, and enabled trade relations to have commenced with the wealthiest part of the Russian dominions.

The reconstruction of Russia, about which the

Foreword

Allies talk so glibly, would have gone forward with a bound by natural means, which not even Allied bungling could have prevented. The Omsk Government could have got money on better terms than any of the Allies, because, accepted within the comity of nations, it could have given better security than any of them, even including America. Europe would have been fed, Russia would have been clothed, and the world would have been saved from its greatest tragedies. All this and more would have naturally followed from the barest performance of our promises.

We did worse than this. Breach of promise is only a negative crime. The Allies went to the other extreme; their help took the form of positive wilful obstruction. The Japanese, by bolstering up Semianoff and Kalmakoff, and the Americans, by protecting and organising enemies, made it practically impossible for the Omsk Government to maintain its authority or existence. The most that could be expected was that both would see the danger of their policy in time to avert disaster. One did; the other left when the evils created had got beyond control. Koltchak has not been destroyed so much by the acts of his enemies as by the stupidity and neglect of his Allied friends.

As the Bolshevik rabble again sweeps over Siberia in a septic flood we hear again the question : " How can they do so unless they have a majority of the people behind them? " I answer that by asking : " How did a one-man government exist in Russia from ' Ivan the Terrible ' to Nicholas II? " Both

Foreword

systems are autocratic; both exist by the same means —"Terror." There is, however, this difference. The autocracy of the Tsars was a natural product from an early form of human society. The Bolshevik autocracy is an unnatural product, and therefore carries within itself the seed of its own destruction. It is an abortion, and unless it rapidly changes its character cannot hope to exist as a permanent form of organised society. It is a disease which, if we cannot attack, we can isolate until convalescence sets in. There is, however, the possibility that the patient during the progress of the malady may become delirious and run amok; for these more dangerous symptoms it would be well for his neighbours to keep watch and guard. This madness can only be temporary. This great people are bound to recover, and become all the stronger for their present trials.

JOHN WARD.

February, 1920.

CONTENTS

Contents

LIST OF ILLUSTRATIONS

WITH THE "DIE-HARDS" IN SIBERIA

CHAPTER I

FROM HONG-KONG TO SIBERIA

THE 25th Battalion of the Middlesex Regiment had already such a record of travel and remarkable experiences to its credit that it was in quite a matter-of-fact way I answered a summons from Headquarters at Hong-Kong, one morning in November, 1917, and received the instruction to hold myself and my battalion in readiness to proceed to a destination unknown. Further conferences between the heads of departments under the presidency of the G.O.C., Major-General F. Ventris, revealed that the operations of the battalion were to be conducted in a very cold climate, and a private resident at tiffin that day at the Hong-Kong Club simply asked me " at what date I expected to leave for Vladivostok? "

The preparations were practically completed when orders to cease them were received from the War Office at home, followed by a cable (some time in January, 1918) to cancel all orders relating to the proposed expedition. So we again settled down in our Far Eastern home quietly to await the end of the

With the "Die-Hards" in Siberia

war, when we hoped to return to the Great Old Country and resume the normal life of its citizens.

Things remained in this condition until June, 1918, when we were suddenly startled by an order to call upon the half of my battalion stationed at Singapore to embark on the first ship available and join me at Hong-Kong. This seemed to suggest that the truly wonderful thing called "Allied Diplomacy" had at last made up its mind to do something. After a great deal of bustle and quite unnecessary fuss the whole battalion embarked on the *Ping Suie* on a Saturday in July, 1918.

It should be remembered that my men were what were called "B one-ers," and were equipped for the duty of that grade; but, after our arrival at Hong-Kong, Headquarters had called in most of our war material to replenish the dwindling supplies of this most distant outpost of the British Empire. Very little information could be gathered as to the kind of duty we might expect to be called upon to perform, and the ignorance of the Staff as to the nature of the country through which we were to operate was simply sublime. Added to this, most of the new material with which we were fitted was quite useless for our purpose. Those things which had been collected on the first notice of movement in 1917 had been dispersed, and the difficulty of securing others at short notice was quite insurmountable.

The voyage was not remarkable except that one typhoon crossed our track not ten miles astern, and for eighteen miles we travelled alongside another, the heavy seas striking the ship nearly abeam, and causing

2

From Hong-Kong to Siberia

her to roll in a very alarming manner. The troops had a very uncomfortable time, and were glad to sight the coast of Korea and the calm waters of the Sea of Japan.

At Hong-Kong many of the men, including myself, had suffered much from prickly heat, which had developed in many cases into huge heat boils. It was very strange how rapidly these irruptions cured themselves directly we reached the cool, clear atmosphere of the coast of Japan.

Elaborate preparations had been made for our reception, insomuch that we were the first contingent of Allied troops to arrive at Vladivostok. Two Japanese destroyers were to have acted as our escort from the lighthouse outside, but they were so busy charting the whole coastline for future possibilities that they forgot all about us until we had arrived near the inner harbour, when they calmly asked for our name and business. Early next morning, August 3, they remembered their orders and escorted us to our station at the wharf, past the warships of the Allied nations gaily decorated for the occasion.

At 10 A.M. a battalion of Czech troops, with band and a guard of honour from H.M.S. *Suffolk*, with Commodore Payne, R.N., Mr. Hodgson, the British Consul, the President of the Zemstrov Prava, and Russian and Allied officials, were assembled on the quay to receive me. As I descended the gangway ladder the Czech band struck up the National Anthem, and a petty officer of the *Suffolk* unfurled the Union Jack, while some of the armed forces came to the present and others saluted. It made quite a pretty, interesting and immensely impressive scene. The battalion at once disembarked, and led by the Czech band and our splendid sailors from the *Suffolk*, and accompanied by a tremendous crowd of people, marched through the town to a saluting point opposite the Czech Headquarters, where parties of Czech, Cossack and Russian troops, Japanese, American and Russian sailors were drawn up, all of whom (except the Japanese) came to the present as we passed, while Commodore Payne took the salute for the Allied commanders, who were all present.

Our barracks were outside the town at Niloy-ugol; they were very dirty, with sanitary arrangements of the most primitive character, though I believe the local British authorities had spent both time and money in trying to make them habitable. The officers' accommodation was no better, I and my Staff having to sleep on very dirty and smelly floors. A little later, however, even this would have been a treat to a weary old soldier.

On August 5 I attended the Allied commanders' council. There were many matters of high policy discussed at this meeting, but one subject was of intense interest. General Detriks, the G.O.C. of the Czech troops, gave in reports as to the military situation on the Manchurian and Ussurie fronts. The conditions on the Manchurian front were none too good, but those on the Ussurie front could only be described as critical, and unless immediate help could be given a further retirement would be forced upon the commander, who had great difficulty with his small forces in holding any position. The Ussurie

4

THE 25th MIDDLESEX LANDING AT VLADIVOSTOK, JULY, 1918.

THE ALLIED COMMANDERS IN FRONT OF HEADQUARTERS AT VLADI-
VOSTOK, COMR. PAYNE, R.N., TAKING THE SALUTE.
From left to right—Comr. Payne, the Japanese Admiral, the American Admiral, Gen. Otani
(Com.-in-Chief of Allied Forces).

From Hong-Kong to Siberia

force had recently consisted of some 3,000 indifferently armed Czechs and Cossacks. The day I landed a battle had been fought, which had proved disastrous, and resulted in a hurried retirement to twelve versts to the rear of Kraevesk. The Allied force, now reduced to about 2,000 men, could not hope to hold up for long a combined Bolshevik, German and Magyar force of from 18,000 to 20,000 men. The Bolshevik method of military organisation, —namely, of " Battle Committees," which decided what superior commands should be carried out or rejected—had been swept away and replaced by the disciplined methods of the German and Austrian officers, who had now assumed command. Should another retirement be forced upon the Ussurie forces, it could be carried out only with great loss, both of men and material. The next position would be behind Spascoe, with Lake Hanka as a protection on the left flank and the forest on the right. If this could not be held, then the railway junction at Nikolsk would be endangered, with the possibility of the communications being cut with other forces operating along the Transbaikal Railway and at Irkutsk. Under these circumstances the council decided that there was nothing left but to ask for authority from the War Office to send my battalion forward at once to the Ussurie front to render what assistance was possible. I naturally pointed out that my battalion was composed of B1 men, most of whom had already done their " bit " on other fronts, and that a few weeks before I had had about 250 General Service men in my ranks, but on

B   5

With the "Die-Hards" in Siberia

a blundering suggestion of the G.O.C. at Singapore they had been taken from my unit and transferred to others doing garrison duty in India. I had protested against this at the time, but had been over-ruled by London, so that my command was reduced to men of the lowest category. However, after making this statement I informed the council that in view of the desperate circumstances in which the Ussurie force was placed I would render every assistance in my power.

About 2 P.M. Commodore Payne, R.N., came to my quarters and showed me a paraphrased cable he had received from the War Office. The cable authorised the immediate dispatch of half my battalion to the front, subject to the approval of the commanding officer. It seems to me they might have plucked up courage enough to decide the matter for themselves, instead of putting the responsibility upon the local commander. As it was left to me, however, I gave the necessary orders at once. That very night, August 5, I marched through Vladivostok to entrain my detachment. It consisted of 500 fully equipped infantry and a machine-gun section of forty-three men with four heavy-type maxims. Leaving my second in command, Major F. J. Browne, in charge of the Base, I marched with the men with full pack. The four miles, over heavy, dirty roads, were covered in fair time, though many of the men became very exhausted, and at the end of the march I found myself carrying four rifles. while other officers carried packs in addition to their own kit.

The train was composed of the usual hopeless-

From Hong-Kong to Siberia

looking Russian cattle-trucks for the men, with tiers of planks for resting and sleeping on. A dirty second-class car was provided for the Commanding Officer and his Staff, and a well-lighted first-class bogey car of eight compartments for the British Military Representative, who was merely travelling up to see the sights. When I got to the front I found a first-class car retained by every little officer who commanded a dozen Cossacks, but I proudly raised the Union Jack, to denote the British Headquarters, on the dirtiest and most dilapidated second-class contraption that could be found on the line. But of course we meant business; we were not out for pleasure.

I was advised before I started from Vladivostok that Nikolsk, the junction of the Manchurian and Central Siberian Railways, was the most important strategical point on the South Siberian end of the line, and that though the position on the Ussurie was pretty hopeless and retirement might take place at any moment, we were not in any circumstances to retire below Nikolsk. The place to which we were to retire and take up a new position had been already decided—a line just below Spascoe, with Lake Hanka on the left and a line of forest-covered mountains on the right.

We arrived at Nikolsk in the early morning, but the platform was crowded with inhabitants and two guards of honour, Czech and Cossack, with band, which mistook " Rule Britannia " for the National Anthem. I was introduced to all the officers, the British Vice-Consul, Mr. Ledwards, and his energetic wife. Breakfast was served to the men by the other corps, and my officers received the hospitality of the good Consul and Mrs. Ledwards. Then a march through the town, to show the inhabitants that the long-sought-for Allied assistance had really arrived at last.

It appears that a very sanguine French officer had travelled over the line some months previously and had made lavish promises of Allied support, which accounts, perhaps, for my previous orders received at Hong-Kong towards the end of 1917. The Allies had decided to make a much earlier effort to reconstruct the Russian line against their German enemies, but, like all Allied efforts, their effective action had been frustrated by divided counsels and stupid national jealousy.

It was the prospect of Falkenhayn, with the huge army of half a million men, flushed with its recent easy victory over Rumania, being freed for employment on the French front, that caused our hurried over-late expedition to Siberia. If the effort had been made at the right time the Russian people and soldiery would not have become so demoralised and hopeless as they had when I arrived, and millions of lives would have been saved from untold tortures. A famous statesman once sternly admonished his colleagues for their fatal policy of doing nothing until it was too late; in this case he himself is open to the same censure.

At Nikolsk had recently been fought an important battle between the Czechs and the Terrorists, and we were shown a series of photographs of horribly mutilated Czech soldiers who had fallen into the hands

From Hong-Kong to Siberia

of the Bolshevik army as prisoners of war. By a section of people at home the Bolsheviks are thought to be a party of political and democratic idealists, but when one is brougĥt face to face with their work they are then proved to be a disgusting gang of cut-throats, whose sole business in life appears to be to terrorise and rob the peasant and worker and make orderly government impossible.

We received equally warm welcomes at many other stations, and at length we arrived at Svagena, which is the last fairly large town before Kraevesk, the station without a town, and very near the range of hostile artillery. Here quite a full-dress programme was gone through by the Czech band and the Czech and Cossack soldiers, ending with a short march past, and speeches by the English and Russian commanders. My speech was made along the lines of my instructions, which were mostly to this effect : We Britishers had entered the territory of Holy Russia not as conquerors, but as friends. The Bolshevik power had made a corrupt and dishonourable compact with their German masters, by which the territories of their Motherland, Russia, had been torn from her side, and a huge indemnity wrung from her people. Under German pressure the Bolshevik Soviet power had armed the released German and Austrian prisoners of war, and by means of this alien force was terrorising the Russian people and destroying the country. The Allies looked upon the Bolshevik power as a mere hireling branch of the autocratic German menace, and as such the enemies of British and Russian democracy alike. We came

9

With the "Die-Hards" in Siberia

to help, resurrect and reconstruct the orderly elements of Russian life, and promised that if they would join us in this crusade, we would never cease our efforts till both our enemies were utterly defeated. And here the soldiers of the two nations made their pact, and though it was not an official utterance it had official sanction. My troops retired to quarters at Spascoe, which I had made my forward base.

Next morning, August 7, with my interpreter, Lieutenant Bolsaar, I visited Kraevesk, and had a long consultation with the commander at the front, Captain Pomerensiv. I personally examined the line right up to the outposts, and eventually it was decided that I would send forward 243 men with four maxims to take up a position towards what I considered to be the threatened part of our right flank. As I was senior officer, Captain Pomerensiv handed the command of this front over to me, promising all help.

Once in the saddle I asked for intelligence reports from all directions, and found it impossible for the enemy to make a frontal attack down the narrow space of the railway, flanked as it was on both sides by impassable marshes. The enemy centre was at Shmakovka, the place from which the Czechs had been forced to retire : that day, however, he had been observed moving a company of about 180 men with three machine guns along the road towards Uspenkie, a small town situated on our extreme right front. After consultation with Captain Stephan, Czech commander, and Ataman Kalmakoff, commanding the Cossacks, I decided to take the necessary steps to destroy this recently formed outpost. Ataman Kalmakoff had that morning announced to me his intention to leave my front and make a wide detour on the right behind the hills, and join his Cossack friends at Iman. I discovered that he was dissatisfied with the lack of enterprise hitherto shown on this front, and had decided to make a raid " on his own " on the rear of the enemy. But the moment I stated my intention to mop up Uspenkie he fell into line, and forgot all about his previous ill-humour. He took up an advanced position at Olhanka, reconnoitred the Uspenkie position the next day, and unmasked the Bolshevik formation, with a loss of two horses and a Cossack badly wounded. I formed my plans on his observations.

My scheme was to advance one company of Czech troops from Khamerovka to Olhanka, the Ataman's most forward post on my right front, where they were to prepare a small entrenched camp. I would also advance 200 infantry with two machine guns the first night from Kraevesk to Khamerovka.

The next day I ordered 200 men to entrain from Spascoe to Kraevesk to act as a reserve. They were to night march to Khamerovka, and occupy the place of my forward party, who would advance by night and join the Cossacks and Czech troops at Olhanka. I would be with the advanced group and make a daylight examination of the post to be attacked, and be joined at night by my second detachment from Khamerovka. By this means I should have had 400 British rifles, a machine-gun section of forty-three men with four maxims, a company of Czech infantry

With the "Die-Hards" in Siberia

of about 200 men, and last, but by no means least, Ataman Kalmakoff with about 400 Cossack cavalry —a total of about 1,000 men. I ordered the two roads along which any reinforcements for the enemy post must pass to be patrolled at night and also closely observed during the day.

I had drawn up my plan of attack and the first stage of the operation had actually been executed, when I was brought to a sudden standstill by a piece of fussy interference.

There was no linguist in my battalion capable of speaking Russian sufficiently well for my purpose, hence I had to seek the services of an agent of the British Military Representative at "Vlady." This agent returned to "Vlady" directly the necessary arrangements for the attack had been completed. I ought to have compelled him to remain with me, but as he appeared to favour the proposed forward movement I did not scent any danger to my purely defensive policy. He did not wait until he had reported to the Military Representative, but when only half way telegraphed from Nikolsk warning me that in his opinion this forward movement should not take place, as he had already received important information which altered the entire situation. I ignored this interference of an understraper, but a few hours later received definite instructions from the Political Representative, that I was to stand purely on the defensive, and not move an inch beyond my position. I was compelled to accept the instruction, but was disgusted with the decision. It proved to me in a forcible way what I had never realised before, how impossible it is for a man at a distance, however clever he may be, to decide a military problem, limited in locality and isolated, as was this case, from questions of public policy. When the one purpose of a force is the protection or maintenance of a limited front, only the man on the spot can be the judge of what is necessary to accomplish that purpose.

My actual plan of operations was very simple. Having assembled my force at Olhanka, I should at dusk have occupied the roads leading from Shmakovka to Uspenkie, and from Uspenkie to the monastery by cavalry, thus making it impossible for enemy reinforcements to reach the post to be attacked under the cover of night. My own troops, together with the Czech company, would have approached the position from the south, and during the hours of darkness have taken up a line within rifle- and machine-gun range. At daybreak fire would have been opened from such cover as could be obtained, and while our eight machine-gunners barraged the post, the infantry would have advanced rapidly on the south front at the same time as the Cossacks charged in from the rear. The result would have been as certain as anything in war could be, and, as since then I have met the Bolsheviks in open fight, I am convinced that this small effort might have had decisive political and military influence in Eastern Siberia. But the " politicals " in uniform are not always noted for daring, and in this case were very timid indeed, and our position grew worse from day to day.

With the "Die-Hards" in Siberia

I made the best dispositions possible in view of my cautious instructions, and soon every man, British, Czech and Cossack, was imbued with a determination to baulk the enemy's eastward ambitions at all costs. The numbers I had brought to their assistance were nothing compared to the influence of the sight of the poor, frayed and dirty Union Jack that floated from my Headquarters, and the songs of the Tommies round the mosquito fires in the bivouac at night. These two factors together changed the whole atmosphere surrounding the valiant, ill-fed and ill-equipped Czech soldiers.

The day following the night I had fixed for the destruction of the enemy outpost two companies of enemy infantry and three guns marched out of Shmakovka as a reinforcement to the debatable position. I watched through my binoculars their slow movement along the dusty road. I judged what the enemy's intentions were, and knew also that I was powerless to prevent them. He quickly placed his guns in position, and the following day sent a few trial shots at Kalmakoff's position at Olhanka; after getting the range he ceased fire. About 11 P.M. the flash of guns was observed on our right, which continued until midnight. At 12.30 the field telephone informed me that the Czech company I had pushed forward, together with Kalmakoff's Cossacks, had been shelled out of their positions at Olhanka and were retreating along the Khamerovka and Runovka roads. I disregarded the imperative instructions I had received from "Vlady" not to move, and advanced my detachment by a midnight march to

From Hong-Kong to Siberia

occupy a position where I could protect the bridges and cover the retreat of our friends. Had I failed to perform this simple soldierly duty we should have placed ourselves in a ridiculous position in the eyes of our Russian and Czech comrades. But though I acted against orders, I think in the circumstances I was fully justified in doing so.

The Czech company retired safely behind the river at Khamerovka, and Kalmakoff's Cossacks took up a new position at Runovka, where he could still hang on to the skirts of the enemy and keep constant observation upon his movements. I retired to a bivouac of branches and marsh grass behind "Lookout Hill," where for a fortnight I carried on constant warfare against infected waters and millions of mosquitoes, without transport, tents, nets, or any of the ordinary equipment required by such an expedition. I admit that my ignorance of the conditions which might be expected to prevail in Siberia was colossal, but so also was that of those whose duty it was to have made themselves acquainted with the situation.

At Hong-Kong I had suggested that we might find tents useful, but the proposal was turned down, either because there was none or because they were considered quite unnecessary. I asked timidly whether I should require mosquito nets, and well remember the scorn with which the Chief of Staff greeted my question. "Who ever heard of mosquitoes in Siberia?" Well, the fact is that while there are a few in the tropics, there are swarms of these pests all over Siberia. In the tropics their size prevents them from doing much damage, except as malaria carriers. In Siberia they take the shape of big, ugly winged spiders, which will suck your blood through a thick blanket as easily as if you had nothing on. They have a knack of fixing themselves in one's hair below the cap and raising swollen ridges round one's head until it is painful to wear any headgear at all. In my case my wrists were puffed out level with my hands. After sleeping, one woke unable to open one's eyes. The absence of any protection wore out the patience and nerves of the men, and the searching Bolshevik shells were accepted as a welcome diversion.

No blame was attached to my chiefs; I was fully equipped as a B1 Garrison battalion, and as such I was dispatched to Vladivostok. I was sent there to perform a certain duty, but on arrival was at once called upon to perform another of quite a different character. I had to carry out the duties of a first-line service battalion with the personnel and equipment of second grade garrison troops. Whether those with whom the order originated in London were aware of the nature of the duty I was expected to perform I do not know; but it is obviously dangerous to send British troops of any category to an actual scene of operations and expect them to stand idle, uninterested spectators of the struggles of their friends. They should either be kept away or sent ready for all emergencies.

CHAPTER II

BOLSHEVIK SUCCESSES

THE outflanking movement by the enemy which I had anticipated from the day I first took over the command, and which I had made my plans to counteract, was now in full swing, but so far no damage to our main position had been effected.

General Detriks visited the front and informed me that the Allied Council had chosen Major Pichon, of the French detachment which was timed to arrive next day, to take over the command of this front. After a personal inspection he expressed himself as satisfied with my dispositions and suggested that I should still retain the command, and that he would see that the decision relating to Major Pichon's appointment was reconsidered in view of the changed conditions he now found. But I could see that a revision of the Allied Council's resolution might affect French *amour propre*, and place both Council and commander in an anomalous position. I therefore requested General Detriks to take no steps to alter the resolution of the Allied Council, and stated that I would gladly serve under Major Pichon or any other commander elected by the Council. British prestige, I added, was too well established for such trifles to be considered when the only reason for our presence was to help our Czech and Russian friends.

17

He, however, pointed out that it was impossible to allow a British colonel to serve under a French major, and that my command must be considered quite an independent one.

Major Pichon arrived on August 18, 1918, and I formally handed over the command. He asked me to consider myself as jointly responsible for the operations on that front, and said that we would from time to time consult together as to any action that might be necessary. I found him both polite and considerate and most anxious to meet the wishes of the several parts of his command; in fact, he was a gentleman whom it was a pleasure to meet and work with. His battalion-commander, Major Malley, was equally urbane, and together I think we made a very happy combination.

The great outstanding personality of this front was Captain Stephan, the commander of the 8th Czech Battalion. Originally a brewer of Prague, he had been compelled on the outbreak of war to join the Austrian Army. He had done his duty as a soldier of that effete Monarchy, been captured by the Russians, and while a prisoner of war had been liberated by the Revolution; he was one of the men who had organised their fellow exiles and offered their services to France and the Allied cause, believing that in the success of England's arms was to be found the liberation of their beloved Bohemia. I asked him why he had offered his services to France, and his answer and his compatriots' answer was always the same : " It is to great England we always look to as our saviour, but the German armies are

Bolshevik Successes

in France, and to meet our enemies on the field of battle was, and always will be, the first ambition of every Czech soldier, for if England says ,we are a nation, we know we shall be."

I must say I felt flattered by the almost childlike confidence which Pole, Czech and Russian had in the name and honour of England. We were undoubtedly the only nation represented on this front and in Siberia generally against whom not one word of suspicion was directed. I naturally expected that the prestige of France, in view of her pre-war alliance with Russia, would be very great, but from the closest observation of all ranks of Russian society I think it would be impossible to say which was most suspected in the Russian mind, France, America or Japan. The presence, however, of French soldiers, and the politeness of the French officers, may do much to generate a warmer feeling in Russia towards France. The presence of the soldiers of the Rising Sun, and the manners and general attitude of her officers towards the Siberian population, will, if persisted in, certainly result in changing fear to universal hate.

On the afternoon of his arrival an important movement of enemy forces on our right front caused Major Pichon to ride through my bivouac, when he was formally introduced to the officers and men under my command. Later he informed me that he did not consider the movement sufficiently important to make any change in our dispositions necessary. Towards dusk Captain Stephan, accompanied by his adjutant, rode up and reported an important move-

ment of enemy forces towards Runovka, our solitary
remaining position on the opposite side of the river,
which formed the natural defence and limit of our
right flank. Again I was asked to move forward to
render such assistance as might be necessary in case
our right were forced to retire across the river. We
marched forward in the darkness with the flash of
the Bolshevik guns lighting up the way, but as their
attention was entirely directed to our outpost at
Runovka, we were as safe as if we had been in Hyde
Park. The Czechs have a fatal preference for woods
as a site for defensive works, and they selected a
wood on the left flank of the road for my position. I
rejected their plan, and chose a position about two
hundred yards in front of the wood at a point where
the roads cross, and a fold in the ground, aided by
the tall marsh grass, almost entirely hid us from the
observation-post of the enemy. Millions of mosquitoes, against which we had no protection whatever, attacked us as we began to entrench, but
officers and men all worked with a will, and by dawn
we had almost completed what was probably the best
system of field-works so far constructed on this front.
How we wished we might see the enemy advance over
the river and attempt to deploy within range of our
rifles! He had by vigorous artillery fire driven
our remaining Czech company across the river,
and so had become complete master of the other
side.

It was here that a second chance came to deal
effectively with this attempt to outflank our entire
position. A sudden dash across the bend of the

Bolshevik Successes

river in the north-eastern corner at Khamerovka on
to the unprotected line of enemy communications
would have resulted in a complete frustration of the
enemy plans, with a fair prospect of his decisive defeat. I even suggested this, but had to confess that
I had moved forward twice, contrary to my imperative orders, and that unless I chose to run the risk
of court-martial, if not dismissal, I could not join in
the attack, though I would come to the rescue. This
was too ambiguous for the other leaders, and the
opportunity was allowed to pass.

Shortly after, I met an old tramp with his pack,
and handed him over to my liaison officer. We could
not very well detain him as he had already in his
possession a Czech and a French passport, but afterwards I much regretted that I had not perforated
his papers with a bullet as they rested in his breast
pocket. He tramped along the road, and my sentries deflected his course away from the trenches,
but he saw my men scattered about in the wood
behind, and at daybreak the enemy artillery began
to spatter the wood with a plentiful supply of shrapnel and shells. One dropped within twenty yards
of myself and officers whilst at breakfast; pitching
just under a tree, it lifted it into the air in a truly
surprising manner. The number of shells—some of
which were German make—the enemy wasted on
that wood proclaimed an abundant supply of
ammunition. To this persistent shelling we had
nothing to reply, and at last from sheer exhaustion
the enemy fire died down. With darkness he began
again, and the feeble reply of three small mountain

guns, which we knew were with the Runovka Cossack outpost, indicated that an attack was developing in that direction.

The unequal duel continued intermittently until 2 A.M., when a field telephone message informed me that Runovka had been abandoned, that the Czech company was retiring across our front, and that Kalmakoff's Cossacks were retiring over the river lower down and taking up a position at Antonovka on our extreme right rear. This meant that our whole defensive positions were completely turned, and the next enemy move would place him near our lines of communication.

This, however, was not our only difficulty. Until two days previous we had been able to give an occasional shot in return for the many sent towards us; then the Bolshevik gunners found the mark on the two guns whose duty it was to prevent an advance along the railway, and our two and only field guns were called in to fill the gap, leaving the infantry without any artillery protection. I cabled to Commodore Payne, R.N., who commanded H.M.S. *Suffolk*, at Vladivostok, informing him of our critical position and asked him to send such artillery assistance as was possible. The commodore was as prompt as is expected of the Navy. In an incredibly short space of time he fitted up an armoured train with two 12-pounder Naval guns and two machine guns, and dispatched it at express speed to my assistance, with a second similar train following behind, the whole being under the command of Captain Bath, R.M.L.I. It is scarcely possible to describe the feeling of relief

Bolshevik Successes

with which our exhausted and attenuated forces welcomed this timely aid from our ever-ready Navy. It enabled us to bring the two Czech guns into position to keep down the fire of the enemy, and gave us a sense of security in that our rear was safe in case retirement should be forced upon us. It put new heart into the men, though they never showed the slightest sign of depression in spite of their many discomforts. The British soldier certainly offers the most stolid indifference to the most unfavourable situations.

The Bolshevik leaders were not long in showing their hand. They remained silent during the following day, but at night they began to shell us from their new position in Runovka itself, selecting as the site for their two batteries the hill on which the Orthodox church stood, and using the Greek tower as their post of observation.

About 9.30 A.M. an enemy armoured train moved slowly forward from Shmakovka, followed by four others, which directed a flank fire at my position The shells all plunked into the marsh about four hundred yards short, affording much amusement and causing many caustic Cockney comments. Next came a troop train which gave us great hopes of a real attack developing on our front, but our Naval 12-pounders on the *Suffolk's* armoured train began to do good practice, and a shot registered on the front enemy engine caused volumes of steam to burst from her sides, and great consternation suddenly appeared amongst the trains' personnel. The Naval gunners did not seem inclined to lose the mark, and so the whole attempt fizzled out, and the trains steamed back to shelter.

The two old Czech field guns, which had been repaired by H.M.S. *Suffolk's* artificers at " Vlady," wheeled into position behind a fold in the ground on our right rear and began a duel with the two enemy batteries at Runovka. This duel was most entertaining. The enemy artillery searched our wood and works, and the line of trees occupied by the French was plentifully sprayed with shrapnel, but they failed to locate our guns, or get anywhere near them, or indeed to cause a single casualty either to man or horse. During the night a peasant gave the guns' position away, and in the early morning exchanges one gun came to grief. The remaining gun changed position, and the duel became still more interesting. By skilful manoeuvring the gun was got much nearer, and at once the range was obtained to a nicety. Every shot was placed so near the mark as to rouse the infantry's obvious excitement to fever heat, and finally a shell was planted right into the enemy observation tower, setting it on fire and burning it to the ground. By placing four shells near to hand, and working like Trojans, the Czech gunners fired four shots so rapidly as to deceive the enemy into the belief that four guns were now opposing them, and after about two hours of this relay work the enemy batteries were beaten to a frazzle, and retired from the unequal contest with two guns out of action. It was simply magnificent as a display of real efficient gunnery. There is no doubt the enemy had intended to make an effort to

Bolshevik Successes

cross the river at Runovka and that his artillery had been placed with a view to protecting the passage of his troops. The young Czech gunnery lieutenant by his stratagem with one solitary field-piece had made this plan appear impossible to the enemy commander. Never was deception more complete.

Having felt our right flank and found it too strong, the enemy continued his movement towards our right rear. He could only do this with safety by correctly anticipating our strategy. He took our measure to a military fraction. He saw that, though he offered the most tempting bait, we made no effort to move forward to snap it up, and doubtless came to the conclusion that we were chained to our positions by either dearth of numbers or military incapacity. In the last stage of his movement his communications stretched for twenty-three miles along our flank, with three posts of just over one hundred men to protect his supply trains. If the commander of that force is still alive he probably has a poor opinion of the ability of his opponents. We were ready to deal him a death-blow at any moment from the day he occupied Uspenkie until he crossed the river before Antonovka. He and his column were only saved by orders from Vladivostok.

For two days no movement was observable in the enemy lines, and it began to look as though he would or could not take full advantage of his extremely favourable position.

I had waged an unequal contest with millions of mosquitoes while trying to sleep in a field telephone hut made of rough branches and marsh grass. The

With the "Die-Hards" in Siberia

Czech soldier who acted as operator had helped me as much as possible, but at last in desperation I got up and walked about until the wonderful colouring in the East heralded another glorious Siberian summer day. The bluey-purple pall had given place to a beautiful orange-tinted yellow such as I had never seen before. The sentry prodded a sleeping Tommy who had a huge black frog sitting on the highest point of his damp, dewy blanket, and a bugle glistening by his side. The sleeper awoke, and after washing his lips at the tank, sounded the soldiers' clarion call, the " Réveillé." Instantly the whole bivouac was alive, but scarcely had the bugle notes died away when the telephone buzzer began to give forth a series of sharp, staccato sounds. The Czech operator gave a sharp ejaculation, like " Dar! Dar! Dar! " looking more serious as the sounds proceeded. He then calmly hung up the speaking-tube on the tree that supported our home and began to explain to my interpreter, Lieutenant Bolsaar, the message just received. It was that Major Pichon wished to see me at his headquarters at once in reference to the serious position of Antonovka. I mounted my horse, " Nero," which was a beautiful present from Captain Pomerensiv on handing over his command, and soon arrived at Kraevesk and heard the full story of the surprise at Antonovka.

From Major Pichon I gathered that Ataman Kalmakoff with his Cossacks had taken up a position on the high ground in the village of Antonovka, keeping touch with the French on his left, and a company of the 5th Battalion of Czechs on his right, who guarded the road to Svagena, and that though he posted sentries in the usual way during the night, the enemy in large numbers crept between them, and when the alarm was given and Kalmakoff mounted his horse he found some thirty of his men already wounded or dead and his machine guns in enemy hands. Most of his troops were in a cul-de-sac, and had to charge a high fence and by the sheer weight of their horses break a way out. Kalmakoff with a few Cossacks tried to retake the guns with a superb charge, but though he got through himself he lost more men, amongst whom was a splendid fellow, his second in command, named Berwkoff, who was greatly loved by us all. A Magyar soldier seeing Kalmakoff with his Ataman banner borne by his side, took a point-blank shot at his head, but he forgot the high trajectory of the old Russian rifle, and the bullet merely grazed the top of the Cossack leader's head and sent his *papaha* into the mud. His banner-bearer could not see his leader's cap so left, and jumped off his horse to rescue it. Raising the cap from the ground, he found himself challenged with the bayonet by the same Magyar soldier. He had no time to draw, but with a mighty sweep, sword in scabbard, he felled the Magyar to the ground; he had no time to dispatch him, and was barely able to get away.

The Czech company was retiring slowly towards Svagena, and the Cossacks, while keeping in touch with the enemy, were retiring towards the railway on our rear. This was a very startling situation, and required immediate action if we were not to be caught in a trap.

With the "Die-Hards" in Siberia

We both decided that a retirement was the only alternative to being completely surrounded.

We there and then drew up the orders necessary to secure that the retreat should be both methodical and orderly. The Czechs were to retire first, past my lines, and entrain at Kraevesk, followed by the English and the French, who were to bring up the rear, which was to be covered by the English armoured train, assisted by the machine-gun section of the Middlesex Regiment under Lieutenant King. So the evacuation of our splendid position regretfully began.

CHAPTER III

It should be remembered that directly it was decided by the Paris Council that a diversion through Russia was the surest way of relieving pressure on the French front, the English apparently decided to be first in. Though Japan was unquestionably in the most favourable position to send help quickly, she was known to have German commitments of such a character as precluded her from taking the lead in what was, at that time, more an anti-Teutonic than pro-Russian expedition. Her Press was, and had been all through the war, violently pro-German, and however much the Tokio Cabinet might wish to remain true to the Anglo-Japanese Treaty, it was forced to make a seeming obeisance to popular feeling in Japan. If it had been only an English expedition, Japan's hand would not have been forced; but the American cables began to describe the rapid organisation by the U.S.A. of a powerful Siberian expedition, which gave the Japanese Government ample justification—even in the eyes of her pro-German propagandists—to prepare a still larger force to enable her to shadow the Americans, and do a bit of business on her own. Several months earlier Japanese suspicions had been aroused by the dispatch to Siberia of an alleged civilian railway engineering force to help Russia reorganise her railways, and the immense benefit that this force had admittedly conferred on the Far Eastern populations was acknowledged on all sides. But the very success of American enterprise in this beneficent direction had created in the minds of the Japanese a doubt as to the wisdom of allowing free play to American penetration.

Japan consequently hurried forward her preparations, and a few days after I had taken over the Ussurie command her 12th Division, under the command of General Oie, landed at Vladivostok. He at once established his headquarters at Nikolsk, and his Chief of Staff, General Kanaka, took up his position behind our lines at Svagena, using us as a screen for the deployment of his command, which had already begun.

Major Pichon informed me that he had telephoned the Japanese general at Nikolsk describing the new situation on our front, and asking him to move up sufficient forces from Svagena to protect our right. I went to my wagon to get breakfast. A little later Major Pichon informed me that the Japanese commander had asked us to suspend our retirement as he was moving up from Svagena a battery of artillery and one battalion of infantry, who would re-establish the position at Antonovka on our right rear, from which we need not fear any further danger. In consequence of this message I ordered my men to re-occupy their old positions, and by 9.30 we had carried out the orders of the Japanese commander.

Having got back into our old position, we in-

Japan Intervenes

quired the direction of the Japanese advance that we might, if necessary, co-operate with their movement, and to our utter consternation were informed that the Japanese had not started, had no intention of doing so, and that we must take what steps were necessary for our own safety, but if we retired at all we were to fall back behind their lines and, we suppose, take no further part in the operations.

The first promise of help and its countermanding had placed us in an extremely dangerous situation. We had left our positions once, and nothing but the lack of vigilance on the part of the enemy had enabled us to reoccupy them without fighting. Our movements must have been seen, and though he had not understood them till too late to take full advantage the first time, that he would allow us to get away so easily again seemed to us to be very unlikely. In fact, it appeared as though we had been sacrificed to give a clear field for some manœuvre or purpose which we could not understand.

Our conference was a very urgent one, and for a time Major Pichon thought it best to hang on to our positions and trust to someone making an effort for our relief. Had British or American troops been collecting in our rear, we would not have hesitated a moment to remain, for we should have been certain of immediate help.

We knew that a battalion of Czech infantry had been moved up from Svagena towards Antonovka to threaten the enemy's outflanking columns, and that this battalion had made it a dangerous proceeding for the enemy to close in on our rear. Hence we decided to withdraw certain units to Svagena, and for the remainder to retire to a position at Dukoveskoie and make a new line from the railway through that village, thus linking up with the Czech troops who had marched to our assistance; they would thus become the extreme right of our new line.

This movement would enable the Japanese 12th Division at Svagena to continue their deployment behind our screen, and if the enemy continued his outflanking tactics would involve the Japanese in the fighting whether they willed it or not.

The retirement was carried out as arranged in perfect order, with the loss of very little material and not more than a dozen men taken prisoners. The French were the last to entrain. The whole movement was covered by the two armoured trains under the command of Captain Bath, R.M.L.I. Before retiring the bluejackets blew up the bridge on our front and otherwise destroyed the line in a very workmanlike manner. If we had been supported, the retirement would have been quite unnecessary; it was the result of lack of confidence in our Allies after the first let-down.

The new line was held as follows: On the left of the railway one company of Czech infantry; the two British armoured trains occupied the railway, and a Middlesex machine-gun battery of four maxims occupied the right, while the wooded slope leading to Dukoveskoie was held by the French, and a battalion of Japanese infantry extended beyond the village. The right of the village was very sparsely held by a reduced battalion of the 5th Czech

Japan Intervenes

Regiment and Kalmakoff's Cossacks. The whole force was under the personal command of Major Pichon.

The enemy quickly repaired the bridges and the line, and within forty-eight hours his armoured trains were observed moving cautiously into Kraevesk, my old headquarters. Simultaneously his patrols advanced from Antonovka and came into touch with Kalmakoff's scouts on the right, and three days from our retirement his advanced elements were testing our line from end to end.

On the morning of August 22 the Japanese 12th Division began to move up from Svagena to Dukoveskoie and deploy immediately behind the new line. As is usual in all Japanese tactics, they pushed their right out far beyond the enemy positions, and early in the evening began to envelop his left with their usual wide turning movement. Their right was supported by two heavy batteries, and from the centre, near Dukoveskoie church, their units, now acting as a reserve, were in position before sunset. Large bodies of Japanese troops were in bivouac immediately behind the centre of the village near their headquarters ready to deploy in either direction.

On the evening of August 22 orders were received to push forward the observation post of our armoured trains to a spot indicated, which proved to be six hundred yards ahead of our positions and near enough to be easily raided from the enemy lines. Lieutenant T. E. King, my machine-gun officer, was at the same time ordered to move forward two maxims, with a reduced company of Czech infantry in support to protect this advanced post. The night was enlivened by constant skirmishes between British and Terrorist patrols until about 8.30 A.M., when it was observed that the Japanese patrols on the right had quietly retired without giving any notice of their intention, and that the enemy were in position on the plain for an attack and had already advanced along a ridge to within a hundred yards of the outpost. The movements of the enemy were observable only from the main look-out, from which orders were already on the way gradually to withdraw the party to a position nearer the lines. Before the order could be delivered the enemy attacked. Lieutenant King proceeded to withdraw the guns alternately, working the foremost gun himself, but defective ammunition frustrated his effort. He gallantly tried to restart the gun, but the enemy were now upon him, and he had no alternative but to retire without the gun. The small Naval party in the advanced look-out were practically surrounded, but under Petty Officer Moffat, who was in charge, they managed to get out, with the enemy on their heels. This party was saved by a marine named Mitchel, who, seeing Petty Officer Moffat in difficulties, turned on his knee and faced his pursuers. Their fire was erratic, but his was cool and accurate, and after three or four rounds the Magyars kept their heads well down in the long marsh grass, which permitted the party to escape. The result of this skirmish, however, allowed the enemy armoured train to advance to a point dangerously near our

Japan Intervenes

defensive works, which, with a little more enterprise and determination, he might easily have enfiladed. But though the enemy train had mounted a 6-inch gun our 12-pounder Navals were too smartly handled to allow any liberties to be taken. This was the situation on the morning that the Japanese 12th Division began to deploy behind the new Allied line at Dukoveskoie.

About 3 P.M. on August 23 I asked my liaison officer, Colonel R. Antonivitch Frank, of the Russian Army, to accompany me towards the front line, as I had heard rumours of large concentrations of the enemy, who, elated with this small initial success, seemed determined to dispute our possession of the village of Dukoveskoie. I arrived in time to witness a duel between one of our armoured trains and a rather spirited fellow of the same sort on the other side. The Bolshevik shells would persist in dropping to the right of our train on a road on which Colonel Frank and I were sitting our horses, so we decided to dismount and send the animals out of range, while we boarded the train and enjoyed the contest. One of our 12-pounders went groggy and obliged us to retire slightly, but we dared not go back far, as the Terrorist train had all the appearance of following, and would soon have made short work of our infantry, which were occupying very indifferent trenches near the railway. Captain Bath saw the danger and steamed forward, firing rapidly; shells burst all round his target, and so bewildered his opponent that he soon turned tail and retired to safety. I applied to the Japanese commander, General Oie, through

35

With the "Die-Hards" in Siberia

Major Pichon that our trains, directly it was dark, might be allowed to return to Svagena to shunt the injured gun to the rear train. About 7 P.M., while preparing to return for this purpose, a few sharp rifle-cracks were heard near the centre of the line. These reports grew rapidly in volume, and now became mixed up with the bass " pop-pop " of machine guns. The rolling sound of conflict spread from the centre along the whole right front. Till now it had been exclusively a small-arm fight. At this point the Bolshevik artillery began to chime in, followed by the Japanese and Czech batteries. The lovely Siberian summer night became one huge booming, flashing inferno, terrible but intensely attractive. The silent tree-clad mountains to right and left vibrated with the music of battle, while shell and shrapnel screeched like frightened ghouls over the valley below, where white and yellow men were proving that there is no colour bar to bravery. This din lasted about two hours, and then died away almost as rapidly as it began.

Our trains which had remained to take a hand in the business if necessary steamed slowly back to Svagena, and I turned into my wagon for the night. After the usual battle with the mosquitoes, I fell asleep, but it seemed as though I had only slept a few minutes, when a banging at the door announced a visitor, who turned out to be a Staff captain from the Japanese Headquarters with an urgent message for the Commander of the Reserves at Svagena, who with great ceremony handed me the following order of the day :

GEN. DETRIKS (CZECH) AND COL. WARD AFTER THE
ALLIED COUNCIL. AT VLADIVOSTOK.

A CONFERENCE OUTSIDE COL. WARD'S HEAD-
QUARTERS. WAGON.

Japan Intervenes

" To Colonel Ward,
  " Officer Commanding Reserves.
    " Operation Order by
" Lieut.-General S. Oie,
  " Commanding 12th Division,
        " Svagena.

" *August* 23, 1918.

" 1. All enemy attacks were driven back to-day. We gained two machine guns and five captives.

" 2. The Allied troops will attack the enemy, inflicting upon them an annihilating disaster, to-morrow, August 24.

" 3. The Japanese troops will attack the enemy, starting the present line, at 3 o'clock, the 24th, morning.

" 4. The reserve British, French, Kalmakoff's forces, and a few Japanese companies will be under the command of Japanese. Colonel Inagaki will arrive at the north-western side of Dukoveskoie at 2 o'clock to-morrow morning.

           " (Signed) S. Oie,
              " Lieut.-General,
      " Commanding 12th Division."

CHAPTER IV

THE BATTLE OF DUKOVESKOIE AND KRAEVESK

I LOOKED at my watch, and called the Japanese officer's attention to the fact that the time was 1.45 A.M., and that Dukoveskoie was four miles distant. Although he could speak perfect English, he held out his hand and with a profound bow pretended not to understand the point of my observation. It was in point of time simply impossible to arouse the British, Czech, Cossack and Japanese detachments and march four miles in the middle of the night in fifteen minutes; but I had lived long enough in the East to know that the Oriental never sets a European impossible tasks without a good reason from his own point of view. I dispatched orderlies to each detachment with definite instructions to be ready to move at once. The Japanese refused to move or even get out of their tents. The Czechs were enjoying a much-needed rest, and refused to budge, while Kalmakoff's Cossacks remained asleep beside their horses. Ataman Kalmakoff was at Vladivostok, and his second in command was dismissed on his return for refusing to obey my orders, as the Ataman was most anxious that his men should be always in the fighting line wherever it might be. Captain Clark, M.C., reported the 25th Middlesex

The Battle of Dukoveskoie and Kraevesk

as ready to march, transport and all complete, twenty-five minutes after receiving the order.

To make doubly sure there was no mistake, I called personally upon the Japanese officer, who point-blank refused either to arouse or move his men in accordance with his own Headquarters' order. I am bound to admit that from that moment I had a suspicion that the order of General Oie was so much Japanese camouflage, and that it was not intended that we should take any part in the immediate operations. I also determined to frustrate this attempt to exclude the Allies from participation, and gave the order to my own men to move.

Our road for about two miles lay alongside the railway, after which the soddened nature of the ground and the danger of losing direction in the darkness forced me to take to the railway. About a mile and a half along the track brought us to our armoured trains, where we were to pick up our Machine-Gun Section, which was to act with us if necessary, or remain as a reserve or rallying-point in case of need. Except for the sentries, the train crews were asleep, and almost within rifle range of our place of assembly. I halted my men and roused Captain Bath to inquire if he had received instructions as to his part in the coming battle. He informed me that he had received a telephone message from General Oie (through Major Pichon) which he could not understand and had asked for it to be repeated. He thereupon produced the message, which was to the effect that a battle would commence at 3 A.M., but that the British armoured trains and the British troops were not to be allowed to take any part in the impending engagement. On the production of the actual message I began to understand why the order of battle had been given to me too late for me to be at the rendezvous with Colonel Inagaki, and the refusal of the units of my command to march with me. These instructions to Captain Bath from the Japanese Headquarters explained the riddle. I gave Captain Bath instructions to move forward in my support in case of need and to watch the proceedings generally, to render aid to any Allied detachment which might be in difficulties, and otherwise to obey General Oie's orders. This duty he performed with complete satisfaction to the commanders of the French and Czech detachments.

Having arranged my rear, the men of the 25th were ordered to move forward in file on each side of the railway track to the point selected for our rendezvous. The time was now 3.25 A.M., the dull light of dawning day enabling us to distinguish moving objects four hundred yards away. A scout came back to report the presence of cavalry on the left, but in the early morning haze we could not make out whether it was friendly or enemy. I moved my troops to the opposite side of the railway embankment and prepared to receive their charge. I then dispatched my liaison officer, Colonel Frank, forward to discover their strength and character. He quickly returned with the information that the cavalry was Japanese, moving into position on our extreme left. I re-formed my men and advanced towards my position as ordered, ninety minutes behind

The Battle of Dukoveskoie and Kraevesk

time. I halted and examined the ground, but saw nothing of Colonel Inagaki or any of the detachments on the spot selected for our assembly. Standing on the line, I saw the foremost enemy armoured train about four hundred yards ahead, and their outpost giving the alarm. No shot had so far been fired, but I gave the order to load. At this stage an incident happened which put an end to the hitherto silent advance of the attacking army. In the act of loading a rifle went off accidentally. The soldier to whom it belonged was standing just behind me, and I ordered Captain Browne to examine and report. In doing so the rifle again went off; it saved the man from punishment, but it began the battle. There was a puff of white smoke, and an instant later a 5-inch shell burst over our heads. The men opened out into the corn and scrub, and I dismounted while the advance continued. Taking my servant's rifle, I led the way.

The enemy must have anticipated our rendezvous, for the place was ploughed with shells from end to end. The first pitched just under the centre of a peasant's cottage, and in a moment cottage and peasant were no more. The heavy purple pall hung on the ground, and had we been on the spot selected, this description would have been written by other hands than mine. By the increasing light and the aid of my glasses I was able to make out the entire scheme of the advance, which was a continuous line from one mile on the left of the railway, extending to about ten miles on our right. A space of about one hundred yards on each side of the line was unoccupied—for the reason, as I afterwards learnt, that it was considered too exposed and dangerous for the purpose of an advance. Unable to find any-one to direct my movements, on my own initiative I decided to fill this vacant space, so making the line continuous, and move forward with the Japanese to the attack. Disposing my men in the shelter of the scrub on either side of the railway, I directed their movements from the centre of the track. There was an ugly moment when a maxim situated in a cornfield began to fire point-blank at a range of one hundred yards, but a Czech outpost entrenched quite near made it so hot for the gunner that after firing about 150 rounds he scooted, leaving a well-placed gun and 5,000 rounds, all belted, behind. We now advanced over the Czech and French trenches, for these forces, like our armoured trains, had been ordered to take no part in the advance. It was while near these trenches that a grey-coated Magyar, four hundred yards away, took deliberate standing aim at myself. It was a most difficult shot, and I felt quite safe, but though the Magyar missed me, he killed a Czech soldier five yards to the left, the bullet enter-ing the centre of his forehead just over the nose. About sixty shots answered his, and he sank across the rails. When we reached him he lay, with many others, quite dead. Captain Clark picked up his rifle and bandolier, and used it with good effect upon the retreating enemy.

There is no doubt that if we had failed to get into position under the cover of darkness we should have had the greatest difficulty in making any head-

The Battle of Dukoveskoie and Kraevesk

way along the railway except with very heavy casualties. As I have stated previously, the end car of the enemy armoured train had a 6-inch gun, but it was mounted so high that the whole platform could be swept with rifle-fire. The reason for the high mounting was to enable two machine guns to be worked along the track from the bed of the car under the heavy gun. If our advance had been observed the enemy would easily have smashed it, but we got within 400 yards before they knew we were there. By concentrating all our fire on the end of the car we swept the platform clear, perforated the body underneath with a hail of bullets so that nothing could live, and put every gun which could be brought to bear along the track out of action. By this means the apparently most dangerous point of our advancing line became the safest, and we accomplished our purpose without a single casualty. Five enemy armoured trains were on the line disputing every inch of the way, but their shrapnel was either too high or exploded so far behind the front line that, though it made havoc amongst the laggards, it had but little effect upon those who kept well to the front. The battle was now joined at all points and reaching the decisive moment.

In the centre by skilful manœuvring, a Japanese 5-inch battery had taken up a position actually in front of the general infantry advance. Such daring deserved to succeed, and in this case it did so beyond all expectations. The point selected was a thin group of trees, which gave a view of the railway from the left, across the plain to Kraevesk, and enabled the leading enemy trains to be shelled almost from the flank. The infantry, while still going methodically forward, were receiving far too much attention to feel comfortable, and Japanese soldiers were putting tufts of grass and leaves in front of their caps to hide the red band, which made an excellent target for riflemen and machine-gunners. Occasionally one would rub a handful of mud around the tell-tale band; experience soon taught the Japanese soldiers the dangers of a little colour. It was just ding-dong open fighting, wonderfully spectacular in character. Then a shell burst plunk under the line behind the two foremost enemy trains, which made retreat for them impossible. Desperate efforts were made to repair the line, but well-directed rifle and light machine-gun fire made this impracticable. Another well-placed shell dropped just under the gunners' quarters on the front train, and instantly the car was enveloped in flames. In turn the fire spread to the gun-carriage, which had become untenable from rifle-fire. This proved a complete catastrophe for the enemy, who from positions on our extreme left and centre had a full view of the slaughter around the doomed trains. Their nerves were completely shattered, their fire became spasmodic and erratic, and then among the trees on a hill to the left appeared a white flag.

That flag was too late. The Japanese cavalry shot out in file as a straight extension of our left. Having come parallel with the farthest group of resistance, they right turned, and instantly swept up the slope in a beautiful line and forward over all resistance, white flag and all. They took no prisoners.

My men were only " B one-ers," and the pace was beginning to tell; still they were leading, owing to the fact that our advance was along the railway and the usual tracks at the side, while the Japanese had to contend with the marshes and woods farther away. I therefore ordered a rally, and advanced only with such troops as could be reasonably expected to keep the line. This party numbered about sixty, and included Captain Clark, the Padre (Captain Roberts), Lieutenant Buckley, my Czech interpreter (Vladimir), Regimental Sergt.-Major Gordon, Sergeant Webb (who, I am sorry to say, died a few days later at Spascoe), Colonel Frank (my liaison officer), and rank and file. With this party we advanced within fifty yards of part of the burning train, amid a shower of debris from the exploding shells stored in its magazine. The second train looked quite deserted, and therefore, beyond examining the ammunition cart of a 5-inch gun left derelict on the road and counting ten rounds of unfired ammunition, we pased without molestation up the railway embankment on the way to Kraevesk.

We had passed the trains and left them about two hundred yards in our rear when we were startled by rapid rifle-fire behind us. On looking round, we were astonished to see spiteful jets of rifle-fire issuing from both sides of the uninjured train directed against thick bunches of Japanese troops who were passing along the track over which we had just advanced. Even the Eastern temperament has limits to its serenity. For a moment the Japs were completely off their guard, but they soon recovered, and dropping flat in the grass, they opened a brisk fusillade. The Magyars were protected by the plated sides of their wagons, and were making sad havoc amongst the soldiers of the Rising Sun. Taking in the situation at a glance, a Japanese officer gave the order to charge. Every man instantly bounded forward, and, like a disturbed nest of ants, they swarmed all over the train, stabbing, clubbing and bayoneting every Bolshevik they could get at, tossing their dead enemies out of the carriages off their bayonets with the same motion as if they were shovelling coal. Then they posted a sentry on the highest part of each train, and the gun in the road, and called them their " trophies of war." My great regret was that no Bolshevik was left alive to tell us the reason why they allowed about sixty English officers and soldiers to pass unmolested at point-blank range of about forty yards, and only began to fire when the Japanese soldiers came under their rifles. Many explanations were given at the time, none of which seemed to be quite satisfactory, so the mystery remains.

It was here that a polite request was made that the British detachment should not keep so far ahead of the other troops, but I was anxious to keep well ahead for an important reason. The Bolsheviks had ravaged and tortured both young and old, rich and poor, male and female throughout the country till their very name stank in the nostrils of the common people. Their blood lust had been so great that when

The Battle of Dukoveskoie and Kraevesk

they had no Russian peasant to torture they fell
back on the poor unfortunate Czech soldiers who
had fallen into their hands as prisoners of war.
Many authentic cases of this kind are so revolting in
character that it is better to keep them in the dark
rather than advertise how fiendishly cruel men can
be to one another. I knew that the Czechs had
threatened to retaliate. The incident of the white
flag previously recorded may have had something to
do with the same sentiment, though I can scarcely
think it had. I decided, however, that the more
humane rules of war should apply so far as I was
concerned, and I soon had a chance of making a
demonstration of my views before the whole army.
A fugitive Bolshevik soldier had escaped from the
Japanese cavalry, and started to make his way across
our left front in an attempt to join the retreating
Bolshevik trains. Exhausted by the heavy going of
the marsh, he had dropped for cover and rest. The
Japanese line was fast approaching the spot where
he had taken shelter, so he raised himself from the
grass and began to run. I levelled my servant's rifle,
but misjudged the distance, and he took no notice.
I took aim at a point over his head, and he dropped
in the grass so suddenly that Colonel Frank thought
I had killed him. As we approached the spot his
black hair showed up above the green, and I took
aim again, but did not fire. I informed Colonel
Frank I wanted the man, if he would surrender, to
be an example of how a prisoner of war should be
treated. Colonel Frank shouted to the man to
surrender. The man shouted back that the Japanese

killed all prisoners. He was then informed that I was an English officer, and if he would surrender I guaranteed his life unless he had committed some greater crime than merely fighting as a Bolshevik soldier. He made no further parley, but almost ran to me as for protection. I was standing on the embankment, in full view for miles, and it was easy for the whole incident to be seen. I took his rifle, with fixed bayonet, and bandolier and fifty rounds from him. His papers showed him to be a demobilised Russian soldier. I placed him under a guard of two men with orders to see him safely to the rear. Time after time demands were made to his guards to allow the murder of the prisoner. But those two British bayonets made his life as safe as though he had been in Trafalgar Square. I could tell by the atmosphere which the incident created that our Allies thought this regular conduct wholly out of place on a battlefield, but it fulfilled its purpose, and surrenders were accepted during the further operations.

Our progress was now very rapid, and except for a few bursts of shrapnel which continued to fly harmlessly over the front ranks and injure such as were far behind, we approached our old station, Kraevesk, easily. As to the method from the military point of view of approaching this place, the less said about it the better. A single company of British troops would have held up the whole show and inflicted losses on the attackers out of all proportion to the object gained. The stuffing, however, was completely knocked out of the Bolshevik army, and the advance

The Battle of Dukoveskoie and Kraevesk

took more the form of beaters driving big game. Having previously reconnoitred the whole ground, I again chose the railway for my party. The Japanese swarmed up through the wooded slope on the right. I chose the railway because I knew the shallow cutting had a slight curve which would give a safe line of approach to the station, situated about three hundred yards behind this low-lying hill. The Japs advanced through the wood in masses, huge bunches of men without regular formation. On rounding the curve, I saw an enemy armoured train about four hundred yards distant. A Bolshevik officer walked leisurely out of our old headquarters and put one foot on the step of the engine, looking straight at myself standing on the line. I drew a bead on him with Lance-Corporal's Moorman's rifle. I do not believe I hit him, but I was near enough to make him skip quickly into the engine shelter. A flash from the leading gun, and a 2-inch shell passed so close to my head that I fell into the four-foot way, and felt the top of my skull to find out if it was still there. This shell exploded about one hundred yards behind me and mortally wounded two Japanese and injured several others. The machine guns on the train now swept the wood, where the Japs were advancing, with such effect that for a few moments there was a regular stampede back over the brow of the hill. My party had taken cover in the scrub on the left, and I crawled on hands and knees in their direction. I found a deep dyke at the foot of the cutting covered with high weeds, and into this I rolled. Gradually raising my head over the thistles, I potted rapidly at the gunner, and my party did the same.

The Japs by this time had recovered from their first shock, and began to open fire on the train, which steamed slowly back to the far end of the station, when it came to a standstill and pumped shrapnel along our front. We had got far ahead of our artillery, so it became a contest of rifle versus armoured train. On the left of the station was a thick log store, and keeping that between ourselves and the armoured train, we crept into the station and began to fire at close range at the gunners, whose heads appeared above the sides of the armoured carriages. The Japanese used a red brick cottage for a similar purpose on the other side, while others tried to outflank the train and cut off its retreat. The officer in charge detected this manœuvre, and, using all his guns, he retired behind the hill, and later was reported as steaming towards Shmakovka. We took possession of the station, and near our old headquarters found a hut in which was the Bolshevik officers' breakfast, with potatoes cooked to a nicety on the fire. These were looted by Colonel Frank and Sergeant-Major Gordon. The sun was very hot—the time was about 8.30 A.M.—we had fought over very difficult country for twelve miles, and as we sat on the crossing of the railway the potatoes were very good. By some hopeless blunder the Japanese cavalry had been ordered to close in from the flank on this station instead of the next, so we lost the huge bag of prisoners which was waiting to be captured. The Jap cavalry commander sat down

The Battle of Dukoveskoie and Kraevesk

and sampled my potatoes, but he lost the culminating stroke of the whole movement. This small minor action proved to be one of the most decisive of the war, as it destroyed the whole Terrorist army east of the Urals.

I was ordered by General Otani to remain in reserve, and returned to my base at Svagena to find the proverbial luck of my battalion had been maintained. The Japs had over six hundred casualties, some of which occurred close to my men, but not a man of the 25th was hit. We had many cases of complete prostration, but, in view of the category of my unit, not more than was to be expected considering the strenuous month's work they had undergone. One and all behaved like Englishmen—the highest eulogy that can be passed upon the conduct of men.

General Oie sent a letter of special thanks to the Commanding Officer of the British unit for their great services in the engagement. At 4.25 P.M., August 28, I received the following communication from the General Headquarters:

" 1. On August 26 the Division had occupied the heights situated at the north of Shmakovka. The inhabitants reported the enemy had left there between nine and twelve on the night of August 24 by eleven trains, strength of which was about 5,000 men; 2,000 men retired by road from Uspenkie. The Division bivouacked at Shmakovka.

" 2. On the 27th the enemy continued their retreat to the north of the River Ussurie, and no enemy could be seen to the south of it, though nine railway bridges out of ten between Shmakovka and Ussurie had been destroyed. Damage done is some ten metres each, and a few days would be required to repair them. The Ussurie railway bridge is not damaged, and on the night of the 26th, after a small detachment had occupied it, one company of infantry reinforced. Against the enemy on Lake Hanka, which was known to have gone down the river with gunboats, one company of infantry has been dispatched to the right bank of Ussurie east of Shmakovka.

" 3. The Division remains at the present position, and prepares to move forward on the 28th."

This completed the Ussurie operations, for the battle was absolutely decisive. The enemy were entirely demoralised, and never made another stand east of Lake Baikal.

COL. WARD AND THE CZECH LEADER (COL. STEPHAN) EXAMINING THE USSURIE FRONT, AFTER TAKING OVER THE COMMAND.

CHAPTER V

THE Japanese, for their own peculiar reasons, as will have already appeared, had decided in the early stages of the operations that the maritime provinces were their special preserve. They looked with the greatest suspicion upon the forces and efforts of the other Allies, especially British and American, and by their orders tried deliberately to exclude them from their counsels and as far as possible from the administration of the territory recovered from the Terrorists. The 27th Battalion of American Infantry had landed at Vladivostok a few days before the battle of Dukoveskoie, and promises were made that they should be hurried forward to take a share in the fighting; but the Japanese, who controlled the railway, saw to it that they arrived a day late. Instead of pushing them ahead, they were detrained at Svagena, and then entrained again from day to day, always about fifty versts behind the Japanese front. In addition the Japanese never trusted their Allies. No order to the Japanese Army was ever given to the Allied commanders until the operation had been carried out or had got to such a stage as to make it impossible for them to take part or offer suggestions.

Captain Stephan (now Major), of the Czech Army, and myself knew every road and track from

B 53

With the "Die-Hards" in Siberia

Shmakovka to Svagena, and were certain that with proper care the whole enemy force on the Ussurie front could have been destroyed or captured. The Japanese would neither consult nor inform any of their Allies about any movement until it had taken place. They treated the Czech commanders with the most scant courtesy; the English officers' carriages were invaded by their private soldiers, who would insolently ask what business we had in Siberia and when did we propose to go home; but they reserved their most supreme contempt for the Russian people. These poor wretches they drove off the railway platforms, using the butts of their rifles upon the women as well as the men, just as though they were dealing with a tribe of conquered Hottentots. I did not understand this behaviour on the part of our Eastern Ally, and felt it could only be the irresponsible bullying of a few individual men and officers. Later on I found it to be the general policy of the Japanese Army to treat everybody as inferior to themselves; they had learnt this Hun lesson to a nicety.

I give two instances which are neither glaring nor isolated, but of which no doubt official record remains. I was standing on Nikolsk platform waiting for a train; there was a crowd of Russian people, and a Japanese sentry was standing near. This man quite suddenly darted forward and jammed the butt of his rifle in the centre of a Russian officer's back; the force of the blow knocked him flat on the floor in such pain that he rolled about for a few minutes, while the Jap, grinning, held his bayonet at the " On

Japanese Methods and Allied Policy

guard!" Though there were many standing near, not one Russian had the pluck to shoot him, and not wishing to mix myself up in the affair, I took no action, but watched further developments. Ten minutes later another Jap sentry repeated the performance, but this time the victim was a well-dressed Russian lady. So cowed were the Russian people that even her friends were afraid to help her. I stepped forward to offer assistance, with the Jap standing over me; when, however, he saw my revolver he put up his bayonet, but continued to laugh as though it was a huge joke. A few Tommies were attracted to the spot, and the Jap saw that things were beginning to take a serious turn. I proceeded to the Japanese Headquarters, situated in a carriage near by, and reported the occurrence. The officer seemed astonished that I should interfere on behalf of mere Russians, who he said may have been Bolsheviks for all he knew, and inquired whether the sentry had ever treated me so. I answered that " the first Japanese that touches an English officer or soldier in my presence will be a dead man." This seemed to surprise the Japanese officer, who pointed out that the Japanese were in occupation of Siberia, and were entitled to do what they liked. I had to inform him that the Japanese were acting in alliance with the other Powers, including Russia; that we were here as the friends of the Russian people, and not as their conquerors. This he would or could not understand. I ended the interview by warning him that if his sentries were not instructed to behave a little less like savages, there would be an end to those sentries' careers. I later heard that the interview did good, but could not in the case of Japanese troops do more than slightly mitigate their behaviour to the defenceless Russian inhabitants.

That is merely a type of their conduct towards ordinary people. There is, however, one excuse for them : given the right circumstances, they treat all alike. A battalion commander was not quite the sort of material to operate upon, for the simple reason that he was usually surrounded with sufficient force to secure proper respect, but a general without a powerful escort was always fair sport for their gentle attentions. Not even the chief of the British Military Mission could hope to escape from the most insulting behaviour. An incident placed my unit in charge of a part of the telegraph system, which enabled me to handle personally the sort of message which entered the Japanese Headquarters relative to a special train that was approaching their station. I handled the message myself. It ran as follows : "A special train, No. ...., will enter your section at .... time ; it conveys the chief of the British Military Mission, General ...., and Staff from Vladivostok to Ufa for important conference with General Surovey, the Commander-in-Chief of the Czech and Russian Armies. You will please give ' line clear ' throughout the journey." Did the Japanese give " line clear " throughout? That will never be the way that this highly efficient and interesting little people will do anything, if their army is a sample of the whole. They stopped the train,

Japanese Methods and Allied Policy

and boarded it with a squad of men with fixed bayonets. They insulted the chief of the British Mission by placing him and his Staff under arrest, and then proceeded to make elaborate inquiries to find out whether they were not German emissaries in disguise. The impudence of the whole proceeding was so remarkable and yet characteristic that when the Staff of the General reported the occurrence to me I did not for a moment know whether I should die with rage or laughter.

I went to Siberia entirely biassed in favour of this admittedly wonderful people. I took care to instruct my soldiers to salute every Japanese officer and to be most polite to every Japanese soldier, and they carried out my instructions to the letter; but my attention was called to the fact that only on rare occasions did a Japanese officer take the trouble to return the salute of my men, and still more rarely did a Japanese soldier salute an English officer. He was much more likely to give an insulting grimace. I say quite frankly that I admire the workmanlike way the Japanese go about their soldierly duties, but it is impossible to ignore their stupidly studied arrogance towards those who are anxious to be on terms of peace and amity with them. It is unfortunately true that they were misled into believing that Germany was ordained to dominate the world, and, believing this, they shaped their conduct upon this awful example. They quite openly boast that they are the Germans of the East. Let us hope that they will read aright the recent lesson of history.

With the "Die-Hards" in Siberia

During my stay in the maritime provinces I never saw or heard of a single act or order from the Japanese Headquarters which would help in the slightest degree in the administrative reorganisation of the country. On the contrary I saw many things which convinced me that the Land of the Rising Sun was at that time more concerned in maintaining disorder as the surest way of fostering her own ambitious designs.

At this stage the other Allies were without a Far-Eastern policy. Their sole object was to push back as far as possible the German-Magyar forces, which were carrying out the sinister policy of Teutonic penetration under the guise of Bolshevism. Bolshevism in the Far East at this date was an attempt to reduce to a system the operations of the Chinese robber bands of the Mongolian border. Mixed with and led by released German and Magyar prisoners of war, they became a formidable force for destroying all attempts at order in Russia and resisting the possible reconstruction of the Russian front against the Central Powers. Previous to the Bolshevist régime these Chinese bands had lived by murder and loot; it was their trade, though hitherto considered illegal, and sometimes severely punished. No wonder they joined the Soviet crusade when it declared robbery and murder to be the basis upon which the new Russian democracy must rest. This German - Magyar - Chinese combination was bound to meet with remarkable initial success. The Chinese got his blood and loot in a legal way without much danger, and the German prisoner played

Japanese Methods and Allied Policy

an important part in the defence of the Fatherland and the destruction of its enemies.

If Germany lost on the Western Front, and by means of this unnatural combination still retained her hold upon the potential wealth of the late Tsar's dominions, she had indeed won the war. This was the reason for our presence in Siberia, but it was not the reason for the presence of Japan.

CHAPTER VI

ADMINISTRATION

SHORTLY after the incidents referred to in Chapter
IV. I received General Otani's orders to take over
the command of the railway and the districts for fifty
versts on either side, from Spascoe to Ussurie inclu-
sive. My duty was to guard the railway and administer the district, taking all measures necessary to keep
open this section of the line of communications. I
was instructed to fix my headquarters at Spascoe,
and make all arrangements to winter there. In
accordance therewith I proceeded to get into touch
with what remained of the old Russian authorities,
civil and military, and the new ones wherever such
had been created. So far as the men's comfort was
concerned, new roads were constructed and old ones
repaired, broken windows and dilapidated walls and
woodwork were either replaced or renovated. Elec-
trical appliances were discovered and fixed, and what
had previously been a dull, dark block of brickwork
suddenly blossomed out into a brilliantly lighted
building and became at night a landmark for miles
around.

We also began painfully to piece together the
broken structure of human society. For over a
year no law but force had been known in these
regions, and many old wrongs and private wounds

Administration

demanded liquidation. I made many journeys to outlandish villages and settlements, with a small personal escort, fixed a table in the centre of the street, and with the aid of the parish priest and the president of the local council, heard and decided disputes, public and private, from threats and injury to the person to the possession and occupation of a farm. There was no appeal—the stolid Tommies who stood behind me with fixed bayonets put my judgments beyond question. I remitted one or two points of property law to legal decision, but all parties in each case protested that they would have preferred my instant judgment. Three murderers I remitted to a court which I called together with an old Russian officer to preside, but he was so terrified at the prospect of having to order their execution for fear they might be Bolsheviks—whose name was a terror to everybody—that I had to send them to another district to enable the law to be carried out. The report of these proceedings spread with such rapidity that it became quite embarrassing, if not impossible, to deal effectively and thoroughly with the daily increasing number of litigants. I began to understand the reason why in more civilised communities legal proceedings are made so expensive. Either the Russian peasant is a most litigious person, or else he mistook a free system of justice as a healthy English pastime which he thoroughly enjoyed.

It was extremely flattering to be told that these people preferred that the "Anglisky Polkovnika Boorpg" should decide their disputes than that they should be reserved for a Russian tribunal. It was the most interesting work I had so far done in the country. The trial of even the simplest case gave me many insights to Russian institutions and character that only years of book study could otherwise have accomplished. I learnt the difference between the right of the peasant holder as compared with that of the Cossack circle. The law of the forest afforded an education in itself. The intimate relationship of Russian family life, from the highest to the lowest, was constantly laid bare before me with all its romance and mediæval trappings and its sordid substratum of violence and superstition. In fact, I became so interested in this work that it was with the greatest regret that I relinquished it for a more urgent and important call.

The Allied forces in the Transbaikal had now accomplished their task of dispersing the forces of lawlessness, and had made some progress in the work of administration, but if this work was to be consolidated and made of permanent value it must be given a centre, other than the Allied command, around which it could rally and to which it might reasonably look for guidance and support. The Siberian Government had been established by the alive elements of the old régime and the more showy members of the Social Revolutionary party, but their authority was ignored and their orders were not often conspicuous for their wisdom. This great people can do almost anything, but even they cannot live without a head, and the question was, how was some sort of head to be provided? The Allies had taken

Administration

control of the far-eastern provinces, but, if their object was to be carried through and German designs frustrated, it was necessary to push at once their control to the Urals and, if possible, beyond. The brilliant feats of the Czechs had temporarily thrown the Terrorist forces into confusion, but with wealthy, helpless Russia as their prize cupidity alone would be sufficient to excite them to renewed effort. To be effective, Allied help and activity must be transferred nearer to the scene of actual conflict, and Ekaterinburg or Omsk appeared to be the only possible centres which could provide the proper accommodation and surroundings for this next step in the Allied programme. This much as a general proposition was conceded by all, but everybody held differing views as to the way in which it should be carried out.

Japan, having firmly planted her feet in the much-coveted maritime provinces, did not look with enthusiasm upon the suggestion that she should leave what she most wanted in order to lessen the pressure upon a front in which she had no interest. That Paris should fall under German blows was of no importance compared with American control of the Chinese Eastern Railway or the presence of the *Brooklyn* at Vladivostok.

America had not exactly made up her mind what particular part of the Far East was most precious in her eyes, but wished to be friendly with everybody and get as much as possible out of all. Her armies were on the Western front, but her eyes were on the Eastern Pacific, and was it not better after all to remain where you could keep an eye on the other fellow?

Who would think of taking a military force over six thousand miles from its base through a partially hostile country? Would it get through the many dangers and difficulties it was certain to encounter on the way? And if it did, who could guarantee a friendly reception? and if not, how could a ghastly disaster be avoided? These were some of the problems which called for decision, and once decided could never be recalled.

The Americans and the Japanese were otherwise occupied and therefore not available, and though it may seem mere national egotism to make such a statement, there was only one force in which moderate Russians of all parties had absolute confidence—without which anything might happen. All eyes turned to the old " Die-Hard " Battalion which had now proved its mettle on land and sea.

Russian society had been ripped up by the roots, and the whole country reduced to a huge human jungle. Human life was at a discount, in fact was the cheapest thing in the country. If a centre of order was to be created anywhere, force must be provided for its initial protection. Statecraft cannot work with violence ever threatening its very life. The risks were great, a big force would create suspicion, a small force must rely upon something more than mere bayonets for its safety. It was with due regard to its dangers, but with a certainty that it was worth it, that I accepted the task which the fates had forced upon me.

Administration

We had settled down for a winter in Spascoe, when I received the necessary orders to proceed to Omsk, with the suggestion that before executing them I had better visit Headquarters at Vladivostok for a conference with General Knox. I tried to get a carriage suitable for the journey for my Staff from the railway authorities, but failed, and ended by purloining a cattle-truck. In this contraption we got as far as Nikolsk, where our truck was to have been hung on to the Harbin Express; but the station-master, the best type of Russian public official, thought it a disgrace that the Commander and Staff of their most trusted Ally should travel so. He placed his private car at my disposal on my promise to return the same if and when I could find another. We arrived at " Vlady," and in four days had completed the arrangements for the move and secured verbal and documentary instructions as to the general policy to be pursued. The means to be employed to worm my way towards the Urals were left entirely to myself.

I had already formed a very high opinion of the Russian character. Much can be done by sympathy and persuasion, but if they fail, then the " big stick " of Peter the Great, used sparingly, is the only method which is certain to secure obedience to orders.

On the return journey I was hung up at Nikolsk for several days. Heavy rains had caused the valleys and marshes to become flooded, and a haystack which had been carried off its bed by the water had lodged against the temporary sleeper buttress and swept the bridge away. The hay had held the torrent back till

With the "Die-Hards" in Siberia

it became so high that it rushed over about two miles of the railway, destroying that also. The Japs would not repair the damage, nor for some time would they give a chance for the Russians to do so. I managed to get orders through to Major Browne so that no time was actually lost. It was estimated that it would take seven days to get on the move, but by a general hustle all round in three days we began our 5,000 miles journey. Starting from Spascoe we travelled to Nikolsk, and then turned back up the Manchurian-Chinese Eastern Railway. On arriving at Nikolsk we were informed that the French Tonquin Battalion had also received orders to move west some seven days prior to us, but were not yet ready, nor were they likely to be for two or three days. We had arrived at "Vlady," and gone thence to the Ussurie front before the French; so now again we led the way towards the sinking sun.

This French unit was under the command of Major Malley, who from his appearance ought never to have dropped the "O" before his surname. He and his officers were some of the best; but the atmosphere of South China had robbed them of some of their native energy. He informed me that his destination was a point on the railway near the borders of North-West Manchuria, and by consulting my own instructions I guessed the object of his move. In case of need I should at least have the border open. In addition to which the move was an indication that so far as this venture was concerned English and French policy ran parallel.

The first part of the journey was through hundreds

Administration

of miles of uncarted corn. As far as the eye could see, to right or left, one vast sea of derelict corn, left uncared for on the land to rot in the Siberian winter. The entire absence of labour, and the complete breakdown of internal administration and communication had produced stark want in the presence of plenty. It made one feel quite sad to look day after day upon this waste of human food and remember the food rations and regulations at home. All along the line there was a continuous stream of refugees of all nations and races—poor, hunted creatures who had horrible stories to tell of the ravages of the Bulgar and the atrocities of the Bolsheviki. At one place the Serbian women and children got the breakfast of my men, the Tommies refusing to eat until the kiddies had been satisfied. And the pathetic homage they paid to our flag when they discovered it was the flag of England! I shall never forget some of the scenes which showed us also the wonderful trust the struggling nationalities of the world have in the power, humanity and honour of our country. It is a priceless possession for the world which Englishmen must for ever jealously guard.

Through apparently never-ending uplands we entered the great range which forms the natural boundary between China and Siberia. On and on, through mountain gorge and fertile valley, we broke at length out on to the wide open plains of Manchuria. Perhaps it could be best described as a combination of all the most wonderful scenery in the world. It is somewhat difficult to keep three huge trains of over forty trucks each together on a single line. This, however, had to be done, first for purposes of safety, and secondly for defence in the then lawless state of the country. The next difficulty was transport. Horses had to be watered, and if they were to be ready for use the train must stop and the animals be exercised every fourth day. Hence much scheming and management had to be exercised for the journey to be successfully carried through.

I saw much about the "hidden hand" in the newspapers we received from home, but our experiences of the same character were sometimes amusing and sometimes serious. The railway was under a sort of joint control, Russian, American and Japanese, and it soon became clear that one or the other of these groups was unfriendly to our western advance. It may have been all, but of that I have no proof. The first incident was a stop of four hours. After the first two hours a train passed us that had been following behind; after another two hours, when slightly more vigorous inquiries were being made as to the cause of delay, we were quite naively informed that the station-master did not think we ought to risk going farther. We soon informed him to the contrary, and again started forward. The next stop of this character was at a fairly big station about twenty hours from Harbin. This station-master held us up for seven hours. This I thought the limit. At last he showed my interpreter a telegram asking him to prevent us going any farther. It was not signed, and when I demanded that we should be allowed to proceed, he said that there were no engines. I had seen two standing idle outside.

Administration

I rushed on to the platform just in time to prevent the engines disappearing. While the station-master had been parleying with me he had ordered the engines to put on steam. I gave orders for my guard to form up across the line at each end of the station and either bayonet or shoot anyone who tried to take the engines away. I then forced the operator to tell me if the line ahead was clear, and threatened to take the station-master under military arrest for trial at Harbin unless he announced my intention to start in that direction and cleared the way ahead. I put a soldier with fixed bayonet on the footplate to see that the driver held to his post and did not play tricks with the train, and started on our journey. We made every inquiry possible, but no one could give us the slightest reason for our stoppage, but seemed to think that there was something wrong with the works which had allowed us to get so far. From then on I took no risks.

There are no special features about Harbin. It is just a conglomeration of houses of a more or less Chinese character thrown together in three heaps, the first two attempts of the thrower not getting quite near enough to the target, which was the junction of the Chinese Eastern Railway. Elaborate preparations had been made by an Allied Committee for our reception, and when we drew into the station about 4 P.M. it was crowded with about as cosmopolitan a crowd of Far Eastern races as we had so far met with—the Mayor, the Chinese Governor and all the notabilities, foremost amongst them being the British Consul, Mr. Sly; but most important of all was

With the "Die-Hards" in Siberia

General Plisshkoff, the commander of the local forces known as "Hovart's Army." Speeches were delivered, and a reply given which elicited from a Cossack band the most astounding rendering of the British National Anthem that was ever heard around the seven seas. The gem of the proceedings was a presentation of two lovely bouquets by the English ladies of Harbin. I never felt so much the necessity for adopting the Eastern custom of kissing all the ladies you are introduced to as at this one supreme moment of the journey; it was a real test of the power of restraint. But the ladies' husbands were there, and everything passed off quietly, even though some wretched fellows took snapshots of the presentation for home production. I inspected the several guards of honour, and General Plisshkoff returned the compliment, while the famous "25th" band discoursed what was declared to be the sweetest music that had been heard in Harbin since its history began. Tea was served in a specially decorated marquee on the platform and all the men were given presents of one sort or another, and the town gave itself over to tumultuous enjoyment, happy in the thought that at last one of the Allies had appeared on the scene, a faint indication that a desperate effort was about to be made by the oldest and most trusted nation in Europe to conjure order out of chaos. The officers were entertained by the British Consul, and preparations were made for a ceremonial march through the town next day. This turned out a great success and greatly impressed the inhabitants.

The day following we were entertained by the

Administration

Chinese Governor, a very courtly old gentleman, and the local Chinese general at the headquarters of the Chinese administration. The band was in attendance, and during the meal dealt with some of the British military choruses which have spread themselves round the world. Of course we all joined in, as only Englishmen can, and this became so infectious that even the staid mandarins unbent and added their quota to the noise. It is surprising to note the resemblance between the solemn Chinese and the self-centred Englishmen. The solemnity of the one reacts upon the other, and both become what neither is in reality nor can be separately. After our hard work and harder fare on the Ussurie this gorgeous banquet was equal to a month's leave, and we let go with a vengeance. What the Chinamen thought about it next morning I do not know; for myself, I only remembered the kindness of this act of friend-ship and the *camaraderie* of the whole affair. How strange that we should feel more at home with these pukka Chinamen than with others we have met who are supposed to have much closer affinity.

Immediately after leaving Harbin we crossed the finest bridge of the whole journey to Omsk. It carries the railway over the River Sungary, which meanders about over the enormous yet fairly well cultivated plains of Northern Manchuria. It is not my intention to describe either the peoples or the countries through which we passed, but no study of the blending and dovetailing of totally different races into the different types that we particularise under the names of Chinese, Mongol, Tartar and Russian, would be

With the "Die-Hards" in Siberia

complete without a journey along the Siberian and Eastern Chinese Railway. The same remark applies to their dress, habitations and customs. It is an education in itself, especially if, like us, one had to stop occasionally to drive bargains, negotiate help, and have the closest and most intimate intercourse with the common people. None of them had even seen the British flag, few of them had the slightest idea where the " Anglisky " lived, and one old Kirghis explained to his wondering tribemen that we were a strange tribe that had broken away from "Americanski " and gone to live on a great island in the middle of the lakes, where no one could touch us unless they risked their lives on great wooden rafts. I thought the amount of inverted truth in this charming description very pleasing if not very flattering to our national vanity.

After climbing the great Hingan Range the plains of Mongolia came as a wonder to me. Imagine if you can a perfectly flat land through which your train glides hour after hour, day after day. The whole is covered with rough grass and a growth somewhat like a huge horse daisy or marguerite. At the time we passed these plants had dried, and a terrific wind sweeping over the plains had broken countless numbers of the dry herb off near the ground. They fell on their round sides. Directly the plants had lost their anchorage away they bounded like catherine wheels over the plains. It does not require much imagination to picture hundreds of thousands of these rounded tufts of dried grass bounding along over immense distances. It is

Administration

quite a fascinating pastime to select a few of the larger and better formed ones coming over the horizon and calculate how long they take to arrive opposite your position. Calculations made in this way convinced me that a small coloured message properly fastened to these moving objects might have been carried five hundred miles in twenty-four hours. If, instead of looking at one, you look at the whole, the impression is of the solid earth passing rapidly from west to east. There are occa-sional obstructions in the shape of a huge flock of sheep which would cover half of Rutlandshire. These are herded by quaintly dressed Mongolian Tartars, on wonderful shaggy-haired horses, who ride at a furious pace around their flocks and guard them from attack by the wolves which infest this part of the world. It is worth recording how they do so. The wolf is a very cunning animal who has numerous methods of attack, and, like a hare, is very difficult to locate if in his form and practically level with the ground. But his very cunning is often his undoing. On no account will the wolf allow a string on which there are little coloured rags fluttering to pass over him, nor will he willingly get near it. The Tartar herds-men go forward in line over the plain in the direction their flocks are feeding with a small strong string with little coloured flags fluttering along it, fastened from horse to horse. This effectively sweeps the whole space as the trawler sweeps the sea. No wolf can hope to escape the trained eye of the Tartar near the horse where the strain of the line lifts it high off the ground, and no wolf will allow the line to pass

With the "Die-Hards" in Siberia

near him, hence the herdsman gets both sport and profit out of his occupation. Having fed off the grass and herbs in one place, the whole Tartar tribe moves forward at regular periods on what appears to be an endless crawl across the world, but what is really an appointed round, settled and definite, within the territorial lands of the race to which it belongs. Their women and children journey with them and hunt and ride with the men, free as the plains over which they travel. In spite of this community of interests the men seem to place but very little value upon their women except as a sort of communist coolie attachment for carrying the camp from one place to another, for preparing the rude meals, and for the care of the boys, of whom the tribe is very proud.

Over this featureless wilderness we progressed day after day, each stopping-place marked by a few aspen trees mixed up with a few others that look very much like mountain ash but are not. The winter houses of the people are single-roomed, square, wooden structures, very strangely built, with flat roofs consisting of about two feet of earth. Against and over these structures in winter the frozen snow piles itself until they have the appearance of mere mounds, impossible to locate except for the smoke which escapes from a few long crevices left open under the eaves of what is intended to be the front of the house. These smoke-escapes perform the double duty of chimneys and also keep clear the way by which the inhabitants go in and out. Their herds are either disposed of before the winter begins

74

Administration

or are housed in grass-covered dug-outs, which in winter, when the snow is piled over them, take the form of immense underground caverns, and are quite warm and habitable by both man and beast. The one I entered had over two hundred beautiful little foals housed in it, and others similar in character had cows and sheep and poultry all as snug as you please. The entrance was lighted with a quaint old shepherd's lantern, not unlike those I had seen used by shepherds in Hampshire when I was a boy. The entrance was guarded all night by a number of dogs, and curled up in a special nook was the herdsman, with a gun of a kind long since discarded in Europe. Such are the conditions under which these people live half the year, but they make up for this underground life when in April they start their cattle on the move by first allowing them to eat their shelters.

Near the edge of this plain we began to encounter a few sand dunes with outcrops, very similar to those on the coast line of our own country. Over these we gently ran day after day until we could see vast fields of sand and scrub that it must have taken thousands of years of gale and hurricane to deposit in the quaint pyramidal fashion in which they stand to-day. Even yet they are not fixed; occasionally a tree falls exposing the naked sand to the action of the wind, which swirls around the hole and moves the sand into a spiral whirlpool, lifting and carrying it away to be deposited again on the lea side of a distant valley, choking the pines and silver birch and sometimes destroying large woods and forests.

With the " Die-Hards " in Siberia

It is surprising that though we travelled for hundreds of miles along the edge of this huge sand plateau we did not see a single rivulet or stream coming from its direction, though there were the traces of a river far out on the plain. Sunset on these sand-hills was quite entrancing. The occasional break in these conical formations, when the sun was low down, gave one the impression of a vast collection of human habitations, with gable ends to the highest of the buildings. The fact is, however, that, so far as we saw or could make out, no human habitation exists over the whole face of this sea of sand, though men live quite calmly around the craters of volcanoes and other equally dangerous and impossible places. The fear created by legends of human disaster attaching to the local history of these sands is of such a character that even the daring of the Tartar is for once mastered. The sands themselves when on the move are dangerous enough, but their cup-like formation would hide armies until the traveller was in their midst, when retreat would be impossible. The same applies with greater force to the banditti or beasts of the desert; hence the gloomy history and legends of the Mongolian sands.

We arrived at Hazelar on a Saturday evening, and collected our echelons during the night. On Sunday morning I made application to the priest for permission to hold our parade service in the grounds of the Greek church. This was granted, and the parade was a huge success. The spectacle of the padre (Captain Roberts) in his surplice conducting the English service under the shadow of the church

Administration

our help had rescued from the violence of the Terrorists was very impressive. The service was watched with intense interest by hundreds of Russian men and women and by crowds of Chinese, Korean and Tartar plainsmen. Some of the Russian ladies joined in the responses, and many women's voices joined in the old English hymns. These were the first religious services that had been held for a year, and seemed to give assurance to the people that their troubles were nearly over, that peace had come again. The huge padlock and chain upon the church door had been removed, and general thankfulness seemed to be the predominant feeling. The scene was doubtless very strange to those unaccustomed to united worship by both priest and people. In these small matters I was extremely punctilious, as I saw what an impressionable people I had to deal with. I further calculated that once we had joined in public service together the edge of hostility would lose its sharpness. I did not leave it at this, but entered the markets without a guard and held conferences with both peasant and workman, stating our reasons for coming and the friendly service we wished to perform. It was clear from the beginning that my safety depended upon our securing the confidence of the majority of the people. A mere military parade would have failed, but with a thorough understanding of our object in entering so far into their country we gained their confidence and enlisted their help. On the other hand, there is a small proportion of disgruntled and abnormal people in all communities who cannot be controlled by reason, and for whom force is the only argument, and for these we also made ample provision.

There was not much interest in the remainder of the Manchurian and Mongolian part of the journey until we arrived at Manchulli. This was occupied by the Japanese Division under the command of General Fugi. Here it was necessary to get a supply of fresh bread and exercise the transport. I paid my respects to the Chinese general, who had just lost part of his barracks, forcibly taken from him for the occupation of Japanese troops. I also paid an official visit to General Fugi and Staff and the Russian commandant of the station.

CHAPTER VII

IT was at Manchulli that an incident happened which was much talked about at the time and was given many strange versions. It is quite easily explained when all the facts are known. It was impossible to secure proper travelling accommodation for my officers, either at Spascoe or Nikolsk, but I was informed that such would be provided at Harbin. In company with the British Consul (Mr. Sly) I called upon the manager of the railway at Harbin to secure such accommodation. He was very polite and promised to do all he could to help, but next morning informed me that no carriage was available, but if I could find one empty I could take it. I failed, and reported the fact to him. He could do nothing, but said there were plenty at Manchulli held up by Colonel Semianoff and the Japanese, who laid hold of every carriage that tried to get through this station, and that Colonel Semianoff collected a great revenue by refusing to part with these carriages unless the user was prepared to pay very high prices for the same. If I was prepared to take the risk, and would use force if necessary to secure carriages, I should be able to get them there, and so far as the railway authorities at Harbin were concerned, I could take any two empty carriages I might find.

79

With the "Die-Hards" in Siberia

The weather was beginning to get very cold, and each mile added to our discomfort, and the only accommodation for officers on two of the three trains were cattle trucks. After my official visit I made request for two carriages. The station commandant pretended to consult the Russian and Japanese officials, and then informed me that there was not one available. I told him it was untrue. He agreed that if I could point out any carriages unoccupied I could have them. He went with his register to the carriages I indicated, and he admitted they were idle and empty and I would be allowed to take them. I put a guard on the carriages and thought the incident settled, but nothing is settled for long in the Far East. I made request for these carriages to be shunted on to my trains, and after a two hours' wait went to the station about the shunting and was calmly informed that they knew nothing about the carriages. The commandant, with whom I arranged the matter, had gone home (an old dodge!), and would not be on duty till to-morrow, and that nothing else could be done.

It was reported to me that the reason the carriages could not be secured was that the railway officials of a certain Power had given instructions that no " class " carriages were to be provided for British officers, as it was necessary that the population along the route should understand that we were not considered representatives of a first-class Power. Englishmen who have not travelled much in the Far East will scarcely understand the working of the Oriental mind in these matters. An officer of

Further Incidents of our Journey

any Power who travels in a cattle truck will not only lose the respect of the Oriental for his own person, but will lower the standard of the country he represents, irrespective of its position in the comity of nations. The representative of the Isle of Man, if he travelled in the best style, would stand before the representative of His Majesty the King if his means of transit were that of a coolie. It is doubtless very stupid, but it is true. Your means of locomotion fixes your place in the estimation of the East, because it is visible to them, while your credentials are not.

I there and then made up my mind to act, and if necessary go " the whole hog." I informed the authorities that nothing should be shunted in that station until those two carriages were joined to my trains, and proceeded to occupy the whole station. Up to this point I had neither seen nor heard anything of the Japanese in relation to this matter, but they now came on the scene, and I soon discovered that it was they who had engineered the whole opposition to the British officers getting suitable accommodation, and had spirited away the old commandant who had registered the carriages to me. At first they did not know the correct line to adopt, but made a request that the guard should be taken off the station. My answer was, " Yes, instantly, if it is understood that these carriages are to be shunted to my trains." They agreed to this, and my guards were taken off, having held the station for twenty-three minutes. I had my evening meal, and was expecting to start when I was informed

that the Japanese had now placed guards upon my
carriages and refused to allow them to be shunted
on to my train. I thought this was just about the
limit, and before taking action decided I had better
discover the reason, if any, for what seemed a definite
breach of faith. I visited the Japanese station
officer, and he said that they had just discovered that
these two carriages were set aside to convey General
Fugi to Harbin a few days hence. I refused to
believe that such a discovery could have only just
been made, and I would take the carriages by force
if necessary.

It looked very awkward, and a Japanese Staff
officer was sent for. I sent my liaison officer
(Colonel Frank) to find the absent station commandant who had allocated the cars to me. The Japanese
Staff officer was expressing his sorrow for my not
being able to get any carriages for my officers and
pointing out how impossible it would be for the train
of General Fugi to be broken up by the loss of the
two carriages I had claimed, when in stalked the
old Russian commandant and blew these apologies
sky high by declaring that these carriages had
nothing to do with General Fugi's train; that they
were unemployed, and they were mine. I decided
to strengthen the guard to eighteen men on each
carriage, and offered protection to the railwaymen
who shunted them to my train. The Japanese
soldiers followed the carriages on to my train, so
that we had the strange sight of a row of Tommies
with fixed bayonets on the cars, and a row of
Japanese soldiers on the ground guarding the same

carriages. No officer came to give them open instructions, but the Jap soldiers disappeared one at a time until the Tommies were left in undisputed possession.

We returned to my car to find it guarded by Chinese soldiers. I asked the reason, and was informed that at an earlier stage of this incident a Chinese officer had been to my car with a note to inform me that the great friendship which the Chinese always bore to the great English nation made it impossible for them to stand by and allow their friends to be attacked while passing through Chinese territory. I thanked them for their friendship, and suggested that Englishmen were always capable of protecting themselves in any part of the world, wherever their duty took them; but they would listen to nothing, and remained on guard until my train moved out of the station.

I do not suppose there was at any time real danger of a collision between the different forces at Manchulli, but it had the appearance of a very ugly episode that might have developed into one of international importance. I took my stand for the sole purpose of maintaining the dignity of the British Army. Other incidents connected with this small dispute about officer accommodation, yet having nothing to do with it, made me determined to carry my point.

During these proceedings I noticed my liaison officer in angry dispute with two Japanese officers against a truck carrying the Union Jack as an indication of the nationality of the train. They were

With the "Die-Hards" in Siberia

pointing to the flag in such a manner that I saw at once the dispute was about this offending emblem. When the Japanese officers had moved away I called Colonel Frank to me and inquired the cause of dispute. He said : " I can understand the contempt of the Japanese for our Russia; she is down and is sick, but why they should wish to insult their Ally, England, I cannot understand. The Japanese officers who have just left me inquired where the English commander got his authority to carry an English flag on his train. I answered it was an English train carrying an English battalion to Omsk, and no authority was necessary. The Japanese officers replied that they considered the flying of any other flag than theirs in Manchuria or Siberia an insult to Japan. I told them they were fools, that if the English commander had heard their conversation (they both spoke in Russian) he would demand an apology. At which they grinned and departed." We tried every means to find the two officers, but were unable to do so. This was the atmosphere in which we discussed the smaller subject, and may explain the obstinacy of both sides; at any rate, it had something to do with my determination.

We arrived at Chita without further incident of importance. Bread and horse exercise delayed us one whole day, and inability to secure engines part of another, until in desperation I went with a squad of men to the sheds and forced an engine-driver to take out his engine, I myself riding on the tender, where I nearly lost my sight with hot debris from the funnel, while Major Browne, who stood sentinel

Further Incidents of our Journey

beside the driver, had holes scorched in his uniform. This act of violence secured not only an engine for my train, but for the others also.

I had broken my glasses, and it was necessary to secure others. I walked to the town and called at the shop of a jeweller and optician, with whom we conversed. Other customers joined in the talk, and we were here informed of the murder of the present owner's mother during the Bolshevik occupation of the town. The Soviet Commisar, with Red soldiers, visited the shop one day to loot the stock. The mother, an old lady over sixty years of age who was then looking after the business, protested against the robbery of her property. The commisar ordered one of the Red Guard to bayonet her, which he did. They then proceeded to remove everything of value, locked up the premises with the dead woman still lying on the shop floor, and for several days refused permission to her neighbours to give her decent burial on the plea that she was a counter-revolutionist. It was evident from the appearance of the place that the Red soldiers were pretty expert at this sort of business; but stories like this are so numerous that it is nauseating to repeat them.

The next point of interest was Lake Baikal, or as it is more correctly described by the Russians, the " Baikal Sea." We approached this famous lake on a very cold Sunday evening, and long before we reached its shores the clear cold depths of the water gave evidence of its presence in the changed atmosphere. A furious gale was blowing across the lake from the

With the "Die-Hards" in Siberia

west, which lashed huge waves into fury and foam as they beat in endless confusion on the rockbound shore. Blinding snow mixed with the spray gave the inky blackness of the night a weird and sombre appearance. Our Cossack attendant, Marca, droned a folk-song about the wonders of the Baikal, which, when interpreted by my liaison officer, fitted the scene to a fraction. We put up the double windows, listed the doors and turned in for the night. I was fearful that we should leave the lake before morning and so fail to get a daylight view of this most interesting part of our journey. We all awoke early to find the scene so changed as to appear almost miraculous.

The strange light of these northern zones was gently stealing over an immense sea of clear, perfectly calm, glassy water, which enabled us to locate the whiter coloured rocks at enormous depths. A fleecy line of cloud hung lazily over the snow-capped mountains. The Great Bear nearly stood on his head, and the Pole Star seemed to be almost over us. The other stars shone with icy cold brilliance and refused to vanish, though the sun had begun to rise. And such a rising! We could not see that welcome giver of warmth and life, but the beautiful orange and purple halo embraced half the world. From its centre shot upwards huge, long yellow streamers which penetrated the darkness surrounding the stars and passed beyond into never-ending space. Gradually these streamers took a more slanting angle until they touched the highest peaks and drove the cloud lower and lower down the side

Further Incidents of our Journey

of the mountains. I have been on the Rigi under similar conditions, but there is nothing in the world like an autumn sunrise on Lake Baikal. I stopped the train ostensibly to allow water to be obtained for breakfast, but really to allow the men to enjoy what was in my opinion the greatest sight in the world. Some of the men were as entranced as myself, while others (including officers) saw nothing but plenty of clean fresh water for the morning ablutions. We all have our several tastes even in His Majesty's Army.

Rumour says there are exactly the same fish to be found in Lake Baikal as in the sea, with other varieties which represent ordinary fresh-water types. I do not believe there is any authority for these statements. Sea gulls of every known category are certainly to be found there, and wild duck in variety and numbers to satisfy the most exacting sportsman.

Passing along this wonderful panorama for some hours we arrived at Baikal. The maps supplied to me show the railway as making a bee line from the south of the lake to Irkutsk. This is not so; the line does not deviate an inch from the western shores of the lake until it touches the station. Baikal is reached nearly opposite the point at which the railway strikes the lake on the eastern side. The lake is fed by the River Selengha, which drains the northern mountains and plains of Mongolia. No river of importance enters it on the north except the short, high Anghara; in fact, the rivers Armur and Lenha start from quite near its northern and eastern extremities. It is drained on the west by the famous

With the " Die-Hards " in Siberia

River Anghara, which rises near Baikal, and enters the Polar Sea at a spot so far north as to be uninhabitable, except for the white bears who fight for the possession of icebergs.

Baikal had been the scene of a titanic struggle between the Czecho-Slovak forces and the Bolsheviks, who had in case of defeat planned the complete and effective destruction of the line by blowing up the numerous tunnels alongside the lake, which it must have taken at least two years to repair. The Czechs moved so rapidly, however, that the enemy were obliged to concentrate at Baikal for the defence of their own line of communication. Before they had made up their minds that they were already defeated a lucky Czech shot struck their store of dynamite and blew the station, their trains, and about three hundred of their men to smithereens. The remainder retreated off the line in a southerly direction, and after many days' pursuit were lost in the forests which form the chief barrier between Siberia and Mongolia, to emerge later on an important point on the railway near Omsk.

We stopped at Baikal for water and fuel, and examined the damage done by the explosion. The great iron steamer which used to be employed to convey the train from one side of the lake to the other was almost destroyed, its funnels and upper works being wrenched and twisted beyond repair. But out from every crevice of her hull and from every broken carriage came German and Austrian prisoners of war dressed in every conceivable style of uniform. There was no guard of any description, but they all ap-

Further Incidents of our Journey

peared to be under the direction of a young German officer, who saluted very stiffly as we passed. No doubt existed amongst these Germans (so I heard from our men later) that we were tramping towards Germany and certain death. Not one would believe but that Germany would win the war, and destroy not only England, but also America. They had no feelings about France, nor would they consider her as other than an already half-digested morsel. Quartermaster-Captain Boulton put it to one prisoner : " But suppose Germany were defeated? " " Then," said the prisoner, " I would never return to Germany again." We fell in with thousands of German prisoners who all held a most perplexing view of ourselves. They described us as the only real and bitter enemy of their country. But the same men would volunteer to work for us rather than for any other Ally, because they said we treated them fairly and behaved to them like men, and listened to their grievances. That is something at any rate.

CHAPTER VIII

BEYOND THE BAIKAL

FROM Baikal to Irkutsk is a short run down the left bank of the Anghara. We arrived at Irkutsk about the same time as a small detachment of Japanese troops, who were acting as a guard to their traders and their stores, who usually travel with the army. The Japs have very pretty bugle calls for different military purposes, mostly in the same key, with a sort of Morse code for the different orders, but a Japanese bugle band is the most terrible thing in the world of sound. It makes one either swear or laugh, according to one's taste. They gave us an exhibition in moving off from the station, which everyone who heard will never forget. I was rather surprised to find that the Jap traders had established themselves at Irkutsk, as their headquarters were at Chita, which was also the centre of their agent, Semianoff. Why they came to Irkutsk at all is a problem. It was generally understood that some of the Allies were prepared to concede them only the fairest part of Siberia up to Lake Baikal. Perhaps they had heard whispers of the mineral wealth of the Urals.

Irkutsk, situated on the right bank of the Anghara, is a rather fine old town for Siberia. Its Greek cathedral has a commanding position, and con-

Beyond the Baikal

tests successfully with the Cadet School for supremacy as the outstanding architectural feature first to catch the eye. The town is approached by a quaint, low wooden bridge which spans the swiftly running river. When we saw it the battered remnants of human society were grimly collecting themselves together after some months of Bolshevik anarchy and murder. Whole streets were merely blackened ruins, and trade, which had been at a complete standstill, was just beginning to show a return to life. Putting out its feelers, it had taken upon itself a precarious life not yet free from danger. The 25th Battalion Middlesex Regiment was the only British unit in the country; it had spread itself out in a remarkable manner, and shown the flag on a front of 5,000 miles. In spite of its category it had brought confidence and hope to a helpless people out of all proportion to its strength or ability.

A public banquet (the first since the Revolution) was held ostensibly to welcome Volagodsky, the Social Revolutionary President of the Siberian Council, but really to welcome the first British regiment that had ever entered and fought in Siberia. It was a great occasion, and the first real evidence I had seen of possible national regeneration. Even here it was decidedly Separatist, and therefore Japanese in character; a glorification of Siberia and Siberian efforts, completely ignoring the efforts of other Russians in the different parts of their Empire. Evanoff Renoff, the Cossack Ataman, led the panegyric of Siberia, and the President and the Secretary for Foreign Affairs, a long, watery-eyed young man, joined in the chorus. They were doubtless all well pleased with themselves, and thoroughly enjoying a partial return to the old conditions. Colonel Frank translated in a whisper all that was said, so that I got a good hang to the mental atmosphere of this unique gathering. The toast of their Ally, Great Britain, was the occasion which brought me to my feet. The band played " Rule Britannia " as a substitute for " God Save the King," for the simple reason that though mostly Social Revolutionaries they dared not play a Royalist hymn until they had tested the feelings of their audience. This gave me my cue. I laughed at their fears, and informed them that whatever happened, our anthem, which for the time represented the unity of our race, would be played by my band at the ceremonial to-morrow, and all the Bolsheviks in Russia would not be powerful enough to prevent it. From this I led to the flag, another great emblem of racial unity. I called attention to the entire absence of a Russian flag from Vladivostok to Irkutsk, and asked, " Is this the country of the once great and mighty Russia that a stranger travels over without knowing what country it is? " I suggested that though we had twenty revolutions I could never imagine Englishmen being ashamed of the English flag or afraid to call themselves Englishmen. The translation of my remarks ended in a wonderful ovation, and I thought the band would never play anything else but the National Anthem, which it repeated again and again.

My list of telegrams and messages of every kind and character from every part of Russia

Beyond the Baikal

and the outside world, together with constant repetition of the speech in the Press, indicates plainly that from this day began the resurrection of the Russian soul. Another sign of renewed vigour and life was the fact that from that day the Russian flag (minus the Crown) flew from the flagpost over every big station we passed, and on all public buildings. The Russians are extremely emotional, and I had managed to strike the right chord the first time.

The day following we marched to the square space surrounding the cathedral, and I inspected the newly-formed units of the army. Splendid men with good physique, but slow and stilted in movement. The remnant of the cadets who had escaped the general massacre was there, a wonderfully smart set of beautiful boys, who at a distance, looking at their faces only, I took for girls, much to the disgust of the colonel in charge. It was altogether a fine and impressive sight, with big crowds and the fine cathedral as a background. With the " Present " and " The King " at the end, every man present uncovered, and an old Russian lady knelt and kissed my adjutant's hand and blessed us as " saviours," while the commandant asked for cheers for " the only country which came to our help without conditions." I wonder how that will pan out?

We were entertained at the British Consul's, followed by a concert at night. It was terribly cold, and no droshkies were to be had. We had to walk to the theatre in a blinding snowstorm. At 2 A.M. we started on our last lap.

The sentiments of the people changed completely

every few hundred miles. After leaving Irkutsk we
soon discovered that we were in enemy territory, and
the few weeks, and in some cases days, that had
elapsed since the retirement of the Bolshevik Commissars had left the country the prey of the desperado.
Let there be no mistake, Bolshevism lived by the
grace of the old régime. The peasant had his land,
but the Russian workman had nothing. Not one in
a thousand could tell one letter of the alphabet from
another. He was entirely neglected by the State;
there was not a single effective State law dealing
with the labour conditions or the life of the worker
in the whole Russian code. His condition was, and
will remain, in spite of the Revolution, utterly
neglected and hopeless. He has not the power to
think or act for himself, and is consequently the prey
of every faddist scamp who can string a dozen words
together intelligently. There are no trade unions,
because there is no one amongst them sufficiently
intelligent either to organise or manage them. All
the alleged representatives of Labour who have from
time to time visited England pretending to represent
the Russian workmen are so many deputational
frauds. There cannot be such a delegate from the
very nature of things, as will be seen if the facts are
studied on the spot. The lower middle classes,
especially the professional teacher class, have invented
the figment of organised Russian labour for their own
purpose.

The condition of the Russian workman is
such that he can only formulate his grievances by
employing others to do it for him. Hence there has

Beyond the Baikal

come into existence numerous professional councils, who for a consideration visit the workers in their homes and wherever they congregate, and compile their complaints and grievances. But these professionals always point out that the rectification of small points like rates of wages and working hours are a waste of time and energy; that the real work is to leave the conditions so bad that, in sheer despair, the worker will rise and destroy capitalism in a night, and have a perfect millennium made ready for the next morning.

The poor, ignorant, uneducated, neglected Russian workman is perfect and well-prepared soil for such propaganda. He found himself bound hand and foot in the meshes of this professional element, who did not belong to his class and, except in theory, knew nothing of his difficulties. When this professional element had misled, bamboozled and deserted him, in a frenzy of despair he determined to destroy this thing called education, and made the ability to read and write one of the proofs of enmity to his class on the same principle that our uneducated workmen of the first half of the nineteenth century destroyed machinery and other progressive innovations, whose purpose they did not understand. There would be less chatter about revolution if our people could only understand what it means to go through the horrors that have destroyed Russia and her people more effectively than the most ruthless invasion.

We stopped at a station near a mining village largely peopled with emigrant Chinese workmen.

With the " Die-Hards " in Siberia

We removed the Bolshevik flag from the flag-post, and insisted upon the Russian flag being run up in its stead. A Russian woman told us to go back, and when we asked her why, she said, " Well, it does not matter; our men will soon find enough earth to bury you." But another Russian woman thanked us for coming, and hoped we were not too late to save a country that was sick unto death.

That night we ran into Zema station, where we came to a sudden stop. I sent my liaison officer to find the cause, and he informed me that a body of men were beside the engine and threatening to shoot the driver if he moved another foot. I ordered the " Alarm " to be sounded, and instantly 400 British soldiers tumbled out of the trucks. Taking their pre-arranged positions, they fixed bayonets and awaited orders. My carriage was the last vehicle of the train. I walked forward to find the cause of our enforced stoppage, and was just in time to see in the darkness a squad of armed men leaving the station. I took possession of the station and telegraphs, and then heard from the officials that Bolshevik agents had come to the town and had persuaded the workmen to leave work, to take arms and cut the line to prevent the Allies moving forward, and await the arrival of the Bolshevik force which had retired from Baikal. This force had worked its way along the Mongolian frontier, and was now feeling its way towards the line to destroy the bridge which carries the railway over the River Ocka at a point about three versts from Zema. I placed guards around and in the railway works, engine sheds, and ap-

Beyond the Baikal

proaches, and discovering telegrams still passing between the Bolsheviks and the inhabitants, I occupied by force the post and telegraph office in the town. Orders were issued that all men must pledge themselves not to interfere with the trains, and return to work by 6 A.M., or they would be dealt with under martial law. Two hours elapsed, during which time my other trains arrived, with machine-gun section complete, and the whole force were disposed to receive attack.

The troops surrounded the house of the leader of the movement, but the bird had flown. I found some Bolshevik literature advocating the wholesale destruction of the *bourgeoisie* and *intelligenzia* (I forget which they put first), also 3,600 roubles, which I gave back to the wife, saying, "That is a gift from me to you." This act disgusted the local chief of the gendarmerie, who assured me that it was German money and ought to be confiscated. I had no doubt it was, but then I was English, and a Hampshire man at that. Then the usual teacher arrived and asked if he would be allowed to speak to the "Anglisky Polkovnika." Receiving an affirmative, he entered and began the conversation. He naïvely confessed that if he had known it was an "Anglisky" train he would have allowed it to pass. They had read my order as to their pledge to return to work, and wanted to know what I proposed to do if they did not do so. I answered that after having taken up arms against us they could expect no mercy, and that if they did not obey my orders every leader I could find I would shoot. The teacher inquired if I would allow the men to be called together for consultation by their prearranged signal at the works. I agreed, if they came without arms. Soon after, the most awful sound came from a huge buzzer. It was now midnight, and the air was rent by a wailing sound that grew in volume, to die away into a world sob. Every Britisher there was affected in some peculiar fashion; to myself it was like nothing so much as a mighty groan from a nation in distress. Colonel Frank, my Russian guide, philosopher and friend, ran from the table when the sound began, and paced the car in evident anguish, and as it died away exclaimed, " Poor Russia! " and I had felt the same thought running through my mind. All my men expressed themselves in similar sentiments and as never wanting to hear it again.

My business was to get out of the place as quickly as possible, but to leave the line safe. The small militia force was quite inadequate to deal with a population fully armed. Hence I ordered the surrender of all arms by the inhabitants, and allowed twelve hours in which this was to be done.

Six A.M. arrived, and my officers reported all men at work except eight, and these reported later and asked forgiveness, which was readily granted. I then informed the management that I intended to call a meeting of the men and hear their grievances. The management tried to dissuade me from my purpose, but I at once ordered their attendance in the headquarters of the works at 10 A.M., when I would hear the men's complaints. Promptly to time

Beyond the Baikal

the work finished, and the men crowded to the spot selected. A British sentry with fixed bayonet and loaded rifle stood on either side as I sat at the table, while others were placed in selected positions about the building. I called the managers and heads of all the departments first, and warned them that I had been forced to take this trouble into my own hands, that I intended to settle it, and that if they interfered with the men in any way, either by harsh measures or victimisation, I would place them under court-martial just the same as I would any workman who prevented the smooth working of the railway; in fact, they being presumably more intelligent, would find no mercy. This information caused quite a commotion amongst all concerned. I asked the men to state their grievances. The first workman said he had no economic grievance; his was political. He had been told the Allies were counter-revolutionists, and as such should be destroyed. Two or three protested against this, and said they came out on economic grounds. They said their objection was to piece-work. I tried to get a statement from them that their wages were low, but they would not consent to this, admitting that their pay for the same work was five times what it was in 1917.

I came to the conclusion that it was more of a military movement on the part of the Bolshevik leaders than a strike such as we understand it in England. I gave my decision that the men's leaders were to be tried by General Field Court-Martial. The men's committee then said that they had never had the chance to meet anyone in authority before,

that they were anxious not to appear as enemies to
the great English people, that if I would carry out
no further repressive action against them, they would
continue to work until the end of the war. They
heard that Bolsheviks were approaching their town,
and knew the tortures in store for them if they were
found continuing to help the Allies in their advance
to the Urals. If I would secure protection for them
they would sign an agreement never to strike until
the war in Russia had ended. I believed them, and
the agreement was signed, but I insisted upon
disarmament.

That evening the time limit in which the arms
were to be handed in expired. We were informed
by the local militia that some arms were handed in
voluntarily, but many more remained.

The following morning a train with General
Knox and his Staff pulled into the station. I reported the whole occurrence to the general, and
how I had received and sent forward notice of his
coming and the object of his journey. It was here
that he informed me of the outrage which the
Japanese officers had perpetrated upon him, in spite
of the fact that a big Union Jack was painted on the
side of each carriage of his train.

The inhabitants of Zema were just congratulat-
ing themselves on having got rid of the " Anglisky "
when they suddenly found machine guns in position
ready to spray all their main thoroughfares with lead
should the occasion arise. Sections of the town were
searched, house by house, until the piles of arms
necessitated transport to remove them. Real

BRITISH PARADE AT OMSK.

Beyond the Baikal

sporting guns which could be used for no other purpose, and the owner of which was guaranteed by the
local police, were returned. In some houses dumps
of looted fabrics from other towns were taken possession of, and altogether work for the courts was
found for the next two months.

The echo of Zema travelled far and wide, and
gave the authorities an object-lesson how to tackle
a cancer as deadly as it was devilish. When Kerensky
destroyed the old Russian army sixteen million
ignorant and uneducated soldiers took their rifles and
ammunition home. This was the insoluble problem
of every attempt to re-establish order in the Russian
dominions. The Middlesex Regiment made the
first plunge at Zema, and others soon followed along
the path indicated. We re-armed the local militia,
and we took the remainder of the confiscated arms
to Omsk, where they were taken over by the Russian
authorities for the new Russian army. I wired to
Irkutsk for reinforcements for the local militia, as I
did not think them strong enough to deal with the
possibilities of the situation. The commandant at
Irkutsk wired that he had information which proved
there was no truth in the rumoured approach of
Bolshevik forces, which reply I knew from the experience I had gained in Russian ways merely indicated his determination not to weaken his own
guard.

At midnight I started on my further journey.
About a fortnight later I received a despairing message from the local militia chief at Zema for help; he
said he was nearly surrounded by the Baikal Bolshevik

With the "Die-Hards" in Siberia

contingent, which had suddenly appeared. I took the message to Russian Headquarters at Omsk, and called attention to my wire to Irkutsk and the refusal to protect this part of the line. Later I received a report from the commander of the Russian force sent to deal with the situation. He said that the Bolshevik leader had come into Zema expecting to receive material and military help from the people. He found them disarmed and unfriendly, and determined to take no part in further outrages against established order. He wreaked vengeance upon some of his false friends, and was then surprised by Government troops, who dispersed his forces, killing 180 and capturing 300, together with ten machine guns and 150 horses.

As a rule, Bolshevik contingents were easily disposed of in a town. They usually looted everything and everybody. Officers were elected from day to day, with the result that such a thing as discipline did not exist. Still, had that party arrived when I was in Zema we should have had a pitched battle worth a lifetime, for as it turned out they had many machine guns, while we had only four; but there would never have been any doubt about the result, for though we were only a " garrison battalion," the steadiness of my men under fire had hitherto been excellent.

We had been passing through hundreds of miles of wonderful virgin forests for the last two weeks, with only an occasional opening for village cultivation and an occasional log town of more or less importance. The hills and valleys as we approached Krasnoyarsk,

Beyond the Baikal

covered with pine trees and frozen rivers, looked like a huge never-ending Christmas card. At last we arrived at Krasnoyarsk, a large, straggling town of great importance on the River Yenisei. As we approached we passed miles of derelict war material—tractors, wagons, guns of every kind and calibre all cast aside as useless, there being no place where minor defects could be repaired. Some had no apparent defects, but there they lay, useful and useless, a monument to the entire absence of organisation in everything Russian.

I had suffered a slight indisposition, so Major Browne deputised for me, and inspected the Russian and Czech guards of honour drawn up to welcome the troops on their arrival. I found the town in a very disturbed condition, and as it was necessary to guard the great bridge, I accepted the suggestion to quarter a company under the command of Captain Eastman, O.B.E., in the excellent barracks which had been prepared for my unit. This place had been originally fixed upon as the station for the whole battalion, but important events were happening in Omsk. Our High Commissioner, Sir Charles Eliot, and the Chief of the British Military Mission, General Knox, had already arrived there, and required a guard, hence I was ordered to proceed with the remainder of my battalion. We remained in Krasnoyarsk for two days, and marched through the town and saluted the British Consulate. On the last evening the usual banquet was held in our honour, and is worth a few words because of an incident which created great interest at the time. The guests were made up of many officers and others in uniform, and also civilian representatives of the Town Council, the district Zemstvo, and other public organisations. The usual fraternal speeches and toasts were given, and not more than the usual six speakers attempted to deliver an address at one time. A number of dark-featured, glowering civilians sat at a table almost opposite to myself, men who by their attire and sombre looks appeared to be unsuited to the banquet atmosphere, and out of place amongst the gorgeous uniforms of Cossack Atamans and Russian generals. They seemed to take not the slightest interest in the proceedings except for a few moments when certain of my words were being translated. All seemed bent on the business of the evening and a good dinner, indicating a return to normal conditions. A Social Revolutionary representative of the town delivered a furious tirade, which I could get my officer to translate only in part, but even that part showed me the world-wide division of opinion amongst my Russian hosts.

The orchestra, composed of German and Austrian prisoners, discoursed sweet music during the evening, alternately listening to the fiery eloquence of Cossack and Tartar. A Cossack officer, who had drunk a little vodka, rose and gave an order to the band, but the prisoners only got out about three notes. What was in those notes, Heaven only knows! Instantly the whole banqueting hall was a scene of indescribable confusion. Tartar and Cossack shouted with glee; older Russian officers ordered the band to stop, and vainly tried to silence the disorder. The dark-visaged

Beyond the Baikal

and apparently unemotional civilians threw off their armour of unconcern, and hurled epithets and shook clenched fists and defiance at their military fellow-countrymen. Then they all rushed out of the building in a body, hissing and spluttering like a badly constructed fuse in a powder trail. It was like the explosion of a small magazine. I had no idea what had happened, but took in the full significance of the scene I had witnessed when told that the notes which had acted like a bomb formed the first bar of " God Save the Tsar." A few miles farther on the Autocrat of All the Russias had already met an ignominious death by being thrown down a disused pit near the line dividing Asia and Europe. In death, as in life, he remained the divider of his people.

The trains started off during the night, and on the evening of the next day we arrived at Hachinsk, where a Russian guard did the usual military honours, and a sad-faced, deep-eyed priest presented me with bread and salt, as becomes a Tartar who welcomes a friend. It was lucky for me that I had some little training in public speaking, and that " Polkovnika Franka " could make such excellent translations, or we might not have made such a good impression as I flatter myself we did on some occasions.

At last we arrived at Omsk, the end of our journey, having passed in a zigzag direction almost round the world. A few miles to the Urals and Europe again—so near and yet so far !

CHAPTER IX

OMSK

As Omsk, unlike so many other towns of Siberia, did not care to pay the usual toll demanded by the railway prospectors, it is situated several versts from the main trunk line. To overcome this inconvenience a branch line was afterwards run up to the town itself. The date of our arrival was October 18, and a right royal welcome awaited us. The station was decorated with the flags of all nations, the Russian for the first time predominating. We were met by General Matkofsky, the commander of the district, and his Staff, who welcomed us on behalf of the new Russian army, by M. Golovachoff, Assistant Minister for Foreign Affairs, and the representatives of the municipal authorities and the co-operative societies. The women of Russia presented us with bread and salt, and, generally speaking, the people of Omsk gave us a real Russian welcome. The ceremonial over, the men were taken to the Cadet School for tea and entertainment, while the Russian officers regaled the Middlesex officers at a feast in the Officers' Club. We were introduced to all and sundry, and began to mix wonderfully well. If we had laid ourselves out for it, we might have visited every decent Russian home in Omsk. As it was, we soon became so much in demand that most of us had in a short time

Omsk

formed lasting friendships with a very charming set of people. Their welcome was doubtless tinged with relief at the security afforded by the presence of well-disciplined troops. The wife of a Russian general told me that she felt as though for the first time she could sleep peacefully in her bed. The little cadet son of another officer gave permission for his loaded rifle to be taken from the side of his bed, where it had rested every night since the Bolshevik Revolution and the cadet massacres had commenced. If I understand the Russian character denials of this may be expected, but it is a fact that the presence of those 800 English soldiers gave a sense of confidence and security to the people of Omsk that was pathetic in its simplicity and warmth. However suspicious of each other as a rule the Russians may be, there is no question that when their confidence is given, it is given generously and without reservation. As to its lasting qualities, that has to be proved, but at the time it is something real and tangible, and no amount of trouble taken for one's comfort is too great.

On the date of arrival I had only a few moments for conversation with Sir Charles Eliot, our High Commissioner, on the political situation. I gathered from him and his Staff that a desperate effort was being made to join the forces of the Directorate of Five, which stood as the All-Russian Government and received its authority from the Constituent Assembly at Ufa—largely Social Revolutionary in character—and the Siberian Government, the outcome of the Siberian Districts Duma, which met at Tomsk and was largely reactionary, with a small mixture of Socialist opinion. The English and French representatives were genuinely anxious that a workable compromise should be made between these two groups and a Cabinet formed that would give confidence to moderate Russian opinion, and so command Allied recognition with reasonable prospects of success. This very desirable ambition of the Allied " politicals " had the sympathy of every friend of Russia, but advice is one thing, accomplishment another. It was impossible to expect that the effects of hundreds of years of tyranny and bad government could be swept away by the waving of a diplomatic wand. The Siberian Government was largely composed of the " old gang," Revolutionary and Royalist, and derived its support almost exclusively from the desire of the people to escape further bloodshed; it was guarded by the Royalist Cossack clans, as lawless as they are brave. The Ufa Directorate derived its authority from the moderate Social Revolutionary party composed of the " Intelligenzia"—republican, visionary, and impractical. Kerensky was, from all accounts, a perfect representative of this class, verbose and useless so far as practical reconstructive work was concerned. This class blamed the unswerving loyalty of the Cossacks and the old army officers for all the crimes of which the Tsars were guilty, and had hunted them like rats in cellars and streets during the worst days of the Second Revolution. The officer and Cossack class cursed Kerensky and the Social Revolutionaries for destroying the old army and letting free the forces of anarchy and Bolshevism, which had destroyed the State and had massacred the manhood of Russia in an orgy of violence and hate.

There should be no mistake made as to the apportionment of blame. Kerensky is considered by all classes of Russian society as the cause of all their calamities. They think, rightly or wrongly, that at the supreme moment when the destiny of his race and country ,was placed in his hands he proved traitor to the trust; that had he possessed one-tenth of the courage of either Lenin or Trotsky millions of Russians would have been saved from worse than death.

To combine these hostile and divergent elements into a united party for the resurrection of Russia seemed impossible to me, as it did to one other Britisher, Mr. David Frazer, the *Times* Pekin correspondent; but the " politicals " thought otherwise. That they were guided by the highest motives and that they gave of their very best in the interest of the Russian people no one who has the slightest knowledge of the high personal character of our representatives could doubt for a moment, but they tried to accomplish the unattainable. The most that could be said of their policy is that it was worth attempting. Try they did, and under the influence of the Bolshevik guns booming along the Urals and of Royalist conspiracies at Chita a piece of paper was produced ,with a number of names upon it which seemed to bear the resemblance of a ,working arrangement between these two opposites.

I am writing this within three weeks of the

occurrence, and may modify my views later, but for the life of me I cannot understand the satisfaction of our " politicals " with their work. They "downed tools " at once and disappeared from the scene of their triumph as though the few names on a piece of paper had solved the whole problem of the future of Russia. It would be mighty interesting to know the nature of their communications to their respective Governments. One thing, however, had been done which was fated to have important after-effects. Vice-Admiral Koltchak had been brought into the new Council of Ministers with the title of Minister for War. I had never met the officer, and knew nothing about him or his reputation, and merely lumped him in with the rest as an additional unit in an overcrowded menagerie. Frazer and I had many talks about these events, but we could fasten on to nothing real in the situation except danger.

On November 6, 1918, we were all invited to a banquet in honour of this new All-Russian Government. It was to be the climax of all our efforts and a tangible evidence of the successful accomplishment of a great diplomatic task. I was rather late, and the ante-rooms were already filled with soldiers and diplomats in grand uniforms with glittering swords and decorations.

I watched this peculiar and intensely highly-strung crowd with the greatest interest, and except for one figure—a sort of cross between a Methodist parson and a Plymouth Brother—was struck by the complete absence of personality amongst the people present. The parsonified person referred to turned

Omsk

out to be the Social Revolutionary, Volagodsky, President of the Siberian Council, who had now transferred his love from Siberia to the whole of Russia. But as my liaison officer was repeating the names of those present a smart little energetic figure entered the room. With eagle eyes he took in the whole scene at a glance. The other officers had bowed gracefully to all their friends and gallantly kissed the ladies' hands, while around them buzzed the conversation. For an instant the buzz ceased, during which the brown figure with the dark, clear-cut face shook hands with an officer friend and departed. The impression on my mind was that I had seen a small, vagrant, lonely, troubled soul without a friend enter unbidden to a feast.

The new President of the Council of Ministers, Avkzentieff, presided at the banquet, and as we sat down I found myself at the end of the head table, which gave me a good view of the stranger I had seen in the vestibule sitting second round the corner. The dinner was good, the vodka gave warmth to the blood and made a very pleasant contrast to the " 60 below " outside. Avkzentieff led the speeches. Immediately my mind flew to Hyde Park Corner, and then to the Lyceum stage with Irving in " The Bells." He spoke with assumed sincerity, cutting the air with his hands in the manner that a Cossack sweeps off a head with his blade. He sank his voice and hissed his words in a hoarse stage whisper, while pointing to the ceiling with a dramatic forefinger. In other words, he was the best actor it had been my pleasure to see for a long time—a second edition of his more famous colleague, the futile Kerensky. Little did I dream that within a few days I would beg for this man's life and that the Middlesex Regiment would shield him from eternity.

Then followed a speech by General Knox (Chief of the British Military Mission), who implored all classes of Russian thought to pull together to establish an Army and a Government capable of supporting law and public order, a speech full of patriotism and very much to the point. Then came General Bolderoff, Commander-in-Chief of the new Russian army and military member of the Ufa Directorate. He had the appearance of a big, brave, blundering Russian officer. Not too much brain, cunning, but not clever. I should, however, give him credit for more than ordinary honesty. Later Admiral Koltchak spoke—just a few short definite sentences. Very few cheers or shouts greeted this orator. He seemed more lonely than ever, but presented a personality that dominated the whole gathering. There was the usual passing round and signing of menus. I sent mine direct to the admiral for his signature, and when he automatically passed it to General Bolderoff I said " Neat," and it was returned with the solitary name of this solitary man. I was now absolutely satisfied that the new Government was a combination that refused to mix, and took the most stringent precautions to see that my unit did not become involved in its impending overthrow. I, however, made an important discovery at this congratulatory banquet, namely, that Russia still had one man who was able to rescue her from anarchy.

Omsk

The business of Omsk went on much as usual, but Omsk society became more subdued in its whisperings. Clique countered clique, and conspirators undermined conspirators, while a peculiar tension hung over all.

During the negotiations connected with the formation of this Government a very serious hitch occurred which at one time threatened the whole project with disaster. General Bolderoff was known as a Social Revolutionary in politics. Through him the Social Revolutionaries had practically supreme control of the new army. Avkzentieff and Co., aiming at Social Revolutionary control of all the forces of the new Government, demanded that a Social Revolutionary should also control the newly-organised militia, which were to act as a sort of military police under the new régime. This was resented by the more moderate members of both groups, as it would have practically placed all power in the hands of one group, and that not distinguished for administrative ability or caution. In addition to which, the very claim made the moderates suspicious as to the use for which such power was to be employed. The presence of the Allies and the determination to form some sort of administration overcame these suspicions, and the moderates gave way and left both forces under the command of the Social Revolutionary group.

The Allies were pushing forward supplies intended for the new armies facing the Terrorists along the Ural front, but it was soon discovered that such arms were being deflected from their proper destination. The front line ,was kept denuded of arms and equipment of which it was in greatest need, while the militia in the rear, and under the Social Revolutionary control, were being regimented and fitted out with everything they required. The appeals of the front-line generals to Bolderoff, the Social Revolutionary Commander-in-Chief, fell on deaf ears, and things were getting into a serious condition. Admiral Koltchak, as Minister for War, presented the appeals to General Bolderoff, and backed them in a very determined manner. Bolderoff was equally outspoken, declaring that the appeals from the front were fictitious, and concluded one of these wrangles by informing the admiral that it was not his business; that the Social Revolutionary group had been forced by one of the Allies to accept the admiral as a member of the Government; that they had done so merely to secure· Allied support and recognition, but he would remain a member of the Government only so long as he did not interfere in business from which, by a resolution of the Directorate, he was expressly excluded. Admiral Koltchak thereupon tendered his resignation, but was later prevailed upon to withdraw it so as to keep up a resemblance of harmony before the Allied Powers. He, however, insisted upon making a personal inspection of the front, for which permission was granted, as much to get him out of Omsk as for the proper performance of his ministerial duties.

CHAPTER X

ON November 4 I received a telegram from Mr. Preston, British Consul at Ekaterinburg, asking that a detachment might be sent to attend on November 9 at the inauguration of Czech national life and the ceremonial presentation of colours to four Czech battalions of the Czech National Army. I consulted General Knox, and he having received a similar request from General Gaida, commanding at Ekaterinburg, that a detachment should visit the several fronts over the Urals for the purpose of giving moral support to the war-weary veterans of our Allies, it was decided that I should take the regimental band and a guard of one hundred picked men for this purpose. Both Czech and Russian were sad at the long weary wait between the promised help of England and the appearance of the first khaki-clad soldier on the scene.

All preparations had been made for my journey, and I was timed to start from Omsk at 3 P.M. on Friday. Early on Friday I was informed that Admiral Koltchak, the Minister for War, was also travelling to the Czech ceremony, and, as engines were very scarce, would I allow his carriage to be attached to my train? I readily consented. About midday a further note informed me that the admiral's

own car was found to be full of the wives and children
of his old naval officers, that there were no other
cars, but they hoped to be able to get another by
7 P.M. The result was that we did not turn out of
the town station till that hour. We had only got
to the lower station, less than a mile on our journey,
when the officials informed me that something had
broken on the admiral's carriage which would take
two hours to repair. I felt there was a deliberate
attempt being made by someone to prevent either
the admiral or myself from performing our journey.
At 11 P.M. I walked out to the workshops where the
repairs were being effected, and sat on an anvil until
4 A.M., through a horrible Siberian night, while a
good-tempered " Russky " blacksmith accomplished
his part of the task.

No Russian official would dream of doing a
straight thing if a crooked one would accomplish his
purpose. So " Polkovnika " Frank telegraphed in
my name to all the railway section commandants
ordering them under pain of summary execution to
clear their part of the line and prepare express
engines at each stopping-place ready to haul on to
the admiral's train the moment it came in. We
bribed an old Russian *provodnik* to get us a Russian
flag to fasten on the admiral's carriage, which he
did, and we became the first Russian train that had
dared to carry a Russian flag for nearly a year. We
also had two Union Jacks, and altogether the Russian
officials became suspicious that here at any rate was
a combination of colour to which the greatest respect
must be paid.

Along the Urals

The result was that we finally started on our journey at 7 A.M. instead of 7 P.M., just twelve hours late, and arrived at our destination one hour in front of time. Guards of honour awaited us, and breakfast of a more or less scanty character. A presentation of bread and salt, on a fine wooden dish on which the ladies had painted a picture of the old monastery under whose walls the great Czech national ceremony was to take place. We marched past the building in which the Tsar Nicholas II and his family had been imprisoned and from which they were taken to die. I am anxious not to believe the untold horrors alleged to have been inflicted on the female members of his family, but they are told categorically. It is best to believe nothing one hears in Russia, and what one actually sees is not always what it seems.

We saluted the flag at the Consulate, where our great good comrade and fellow-countryman, Consul Preston, gave warmth and good cheer to man and beast. Suddenly we turned to the right and entered a huge square, already surrounded by Czech troops, infantry, artillery and cavalry. It was indeed a great sight. On the highest corner of the square a platform was erected, on the right of which we were given the post of honour, and for some strange reason which I could not understand were asked to play the British National Anthem, when the whole Czech Army came to the " Present ! " as General Gaida and his Staff, with the colours, entered the square. I felt that we were celebrating the birth of a nation. The scene had that peculiar solemnity about it that makes the moment feel pregnant with world events. One of the units was my old Ussurie battalion, and our old chum, Captain (now Colonel) Stephan, was the proudest man there, as he bore from the hands of the priest the newly-consecrated colours of his country. What quantities of beer we shall drink together if I ever see him in his dear Prague, thinking of our thirsty days in Eastern Siberia!

It was my first introduction to the dashing young Czech officer, General Gaida, who by sheer pluck had played such an important part in cutting a way for his army from west to east. We had the usual banquet, at which Admiral Koltchak delivered the first important speech since his appointment as Minister for War. I gave expression to the delight of my own country at the birth of new nations and the resurrection of freedom amongst the subject people of the world. I also gave expression to my pleasure that the first act of the new Russian Minister for War was to visit his army at the front and make himself personally acquainted with the conditions of the Russian soldiers who were so gallantly fighting to protect the people and the State from violence and anarchy.

The ceremony over, we started at once for the Kunghure front, and the early morning found us sliding rapidly down the European side of the Urals. Huge forests, all loaded with snow, covered the mountain sides, and there was a temperature quite impossible for British military operations. We arrived about 11 A.M. at the headquarters of the

Along the Urals

army under the command of General Count Galitzin. We held long conferences and then lunched in his mess, which was quartered in an eight-wheeled American truck. An occasional shell exploded first to right and then to left, but none came very near, and by 2 P.M. the firing died away altogether. It was decided to march to the advanced outpost and take the band to give both friend and foe an opportunity to judge a sample of British music. We got to the extreme point near which a cutting in the railway gave excellent protection for the band, while the admiral's Staff and my Middlesex guard went forward to have a look at the enemy. The band started "Colonel Bogey," then went on to something which I do not remember, but while we were groping about through machine-gun pits, etc., the band behind began "Tipperary." That just put the finishing touch to Bolshevik patience! This famous war tune got on their gunners' nerves and they began to shell the tune for all they were worth. Needless to say not a single shell went anywhere near the mark. All shrieked over our heads and exploded harmlessly among the forest trees; one, however, dropped near the railway bridge and went off like a Hampstead squib on a wet bonfire night. It shows an utter lack of culture among the Bolshevik officers that they could not appreciate good music after we had taken so much trouble to bring it within their reach. The band finished and the shelling ended. I expect they fancied they had frightened my bandsmen, but the fact was they enjoyed the unique experience immensely.

With the " Die-Hards " in Siberia

General Count Galitzin is a very fine type of the officer of the old régime; an aristocrat to his finger tips, but a fine leader of men, born to command. I should think there is a big strain of Tartar blood in his make-up, but he is altogether the sort of man one would prefer to meet as friend rather than foe. We discussed the possibility of an offensive in the direction of Perm, from where I humorously suggested we might be able to rescue the forces of General Poole, which had gone into winter quarters somewhere in the direction of Archangel. We returned to Ekaterinburg, and without stopping, proceeded towards the Lisvin front to meet General Pepelaieff.

We arrived on the Lisvin front about 10 A.M. next day, but did not see the enemy or hear his guns. This army had been compelled to retire some 60 versts the very day we were discussing an advance on Perm, and its present position was none too secure. Pepelaieff is a young general, not more than thirty, but looked a real hard-working soldier. His uniform was as dirty and worn, though not quite so dilapidated, as the majority of his soldiers. He had absolute confidence that he could beat the enemy if his men had rifles and ammunition, which many had not. Half his men were waiting for the rifles of comrades who might be killed or frozen in the snow. The conferences were quite businesslike, and Admiral Koltchak's presence seemed to galvanise the whole army into life and energy. The " Russky soldat," whose boots had long since disappeared and whose feet were bound up in bags to protect them from the snow, felt almost certain that proper boots and clothes would follow from the War Minister's visit. Pepelaieff came back in my carriage to meet General Gaida, and the admiral also relished a British soldier's ration as we discussed things generally, including the proposed advance and the necessary measures to make it into a victory.

We were to have gone next to the extreme right, where General Verzbitsky operated on the flank, but the admiral said the condition of the soldiers was very sad, and his immediate business was to organise the rear and so secure the means by which the soldier at the front could do his duty. We saw the ceremonial of the presentation of colours to the 11th Siberian Rifles, a fine proceeding greatly enhanced by the fact that three officers of the regiment had rescued the colours (originally presented by Peter the Great) from the Bolshevik Revolutionaries, and as pedlars and peasants had tramped for months through the Bolshevik lines and brought them safely to the new regiment.

It was necessary for the admiral to see General Surovey and General Detriks and their Staffs at Chilliyabinsk, and also to have a look at the Ufa front. Travelling all night, we arrived at Chilliyabinsk next morning, and after quite a formal inspection of guards, we adjourned for lunch. The date I do not remember, but my old friend Colonel Pichon burst through all etiquette to inform me of the terms of armistice between Germany and the Entente, and brought out a bottle of champagne he had preserved for the occasion; we swore by all the powers above and below that we were the greatest people the world had ever seen in all its ages and intended to remain so.

Lunch over, I left the admiral to his generals and walked a little through this straggling, snow-swept town, firmly believing that we were about to start for Ufa. At 5 p.m. I was informed that the conferences were over and there were urgent reasons for an immediate return to Omsk. I did not object as I was not anxious to see more of this army of ill-fed, half-clad soldiers struggling to save the State under intolerable conditions. We started on our return journey and travelled till 11 a.m. next day, by which time we had arrived at Petropalovsk. Here the station commandant informed us that General Bolderoff wished our train to wait for his, as it was most essential that he should have a conference with the Minister for War. This was the first intimation I had received that General Bolderoff had left Omsk and was on his way to visit the Ufa front. The admiral invited me to his carriage and explained the critical situation at Omsk, but could give no reason for the sudden decision of the Commander-in-Chief to leave Omsk and meet him on the way. I had my suspicions that the two groups of the Government had come to grips, and that each had decided to destroy the other ; that Admiral Koltchak was to be sounded as to which of these groups had his favour, and that his life, and perhaps that of his British escort, would depend upon his answer. Bolderoff and the people at Omsk were unaware of the presence of the British escort or its numbers, and while they

Along the Urals

may have discovered our joint appearance at the
Ekaterinburg function, there had been no original
decision to accompany the admiral to Chilliyabinsk.
That was only arranged the previous day. In revolutions you can never be too careful, hence I gave
orders to my men to load and be ready for instant
action if necessary. Orders were also issued to patrol
the platform and allow no people, uniformed or
otherwise, to collect near the trains, and in no circumstances were the two soldiers who were to accompany
the admiral to lose sight of him for one instant without reporting it to me. Two others stood guard at
the entrance to General Bolderoff's carriage. When
I saw the look on the face of the Commander-in-
Chief's attendants I was satisfied that my precautions
were no more than necessary.

The general's train drew into the station and
Admiral Koltchak entered Bolderoff's carriage at
exactly 12 noon on November 6, 1918. I asked my
servant, Moorman, to take a "snap" of the two
trains, as I felt that this conference was full of
big events for Russia. While taking the snap a
returned emigrant workman spoke to Moorman in
good English. He asked who all these officers were
and what they were all talking about, and when my
servant informed him he did not know, the emigrant
said : " It is all right so long as they do not want
to bring back the old régime, but if that is their
object I can tell them that Russia will never submit
to live under the old régime again." I thought, and
think now, that in that workman's words I heard
the voice of Russia. The conference between the

admiral and the general broke up at five o'clock; it had lasted five hours.

The admiral was hungry and came into my carriage for something to eat; his servants had nothing ready as it is the Russian custom never to begin to prepare a meal till you are ready to eat it. After the meal we talked, and from the conversation I gathered the nature of the questions discussed at his conference with the Commander-in-Chief. He asked me whether in England our Minister for War had any responsibilities placed upon him for the supply of clothing, equipment and general condition of the British Army? I replied that in England the Minister for War was responsible to the Cabinet and, through Parliament, to the country for the general efficiency of the British Army in every detail. He answered : " What would you think in England if the Commander-in-Chief told the Minister for War that these matters had nothing to do with him, that he would be allowed to keep a small office with two clerks but no staff, as it was the Minister for War's name only that was of any use to the Directorate (or in your case Cabinet), and the less he interfered with the affairs of his department the better for all concerned? " I answered : " If I were the Minister I should claim to have absolute control of my department, or resign." He thought a minute and said : " That is what I have done," or "what I intend to do," I forget which. From what followed I think it must have been the former, because I asked him what General Bolderoff said in answer to his claim, to which he replied : " General Bolderoff

Along the Urals

is a very good man, and though he does not see everything as I wish, I think he understands the situation, and will himself ask that greater power should be given to enable me to save the new Russian army, that it may be able to resurrect the Russian State." I well remember that word "resurrect"; it was so pregnant with truth. The State *was* dead, Russia was no more; resurrection was necessary.

We arrived at Omsk town station at 5.30 on the evening of November 17, 1918. The admiral thanked me for my help and my guard and for the kindness and protection I had afforded him. I promised him my continued help and sympathy in his patriotic attempt to revive the spirit of his people. He went straight to his lodgings and remained there.

The *Times* correspondent in a message to his newspaper has suggested that the admiral had prior knowledge of what was to happen that night in Omsk. I do not think that was the case. He may have guessed that something very unpleasant was in the wind—the least sensitive amongst those behind the scenes knew that—but what it was, from which direction it would come or on whom it would fall was a secret known to but very few, and I am convinced that the admiral, except in a second degree, was not one of them. Colonel (soon to be General) Lebediff could tell the whole story, though his name was not even mentioned during the *coup d'état*. A young and able Cossack officer, he was on the Staff of Korniloff when Kerensky invited the great Cossack general to march his army to Petrograd to save the newly-elected National Assembly. It is well known

With the " Die-Hards " in Siberia

how, when Korniloff obeyed Kerensky's order, he treacherously turned and rent to pieces the only force which was moving at his own request and could have saved Russia. He, in turn, became the victim of the ghouls who urged him to this act of destruction. Lebediff escaped, but one can be certain that he retained a lasting hate towards the Social Revolutionaries who had betrayed his great leader.

The comrades of Kerensky, and in some cases the actual betrayers, had found refuge in the Directorate of Five and the Council of Ministers, and were continuing to play the same double game which had brought ruin on the first National Assembly and disaster upon the Russian people. They were members of the same futile crowd of useless charlatans who by their pusillanimity had made their country a byword and the Treaty of Brest-Litovsk possible. I was in a position to judge. I was certain that this young man was the wrong sort to allow the execution of his chief to pass without attempting punishment.

He had drifted down to Southern Russia and joined General Denikin in his first efforts against the Bolsheviks. Sent from Denikin with dispatches to Omsk, he became the centre of a group of desperadoes who were in want of a cool brain to make them formidable. The state of Omsk at this time was simply indescribable. Every night as soon as darkness set in rifle and revolver shots and shouts could be heard in all directions. The morning sanitary carts picked up from five to twenty dead officers. There were no police, no courts, no law,

Along the Urals

no anything. In desperation the officers grouped themselves together and hit back indiscriminately at the people they thought responsible for the murder of their comrades. So a fair proportion of civilian bodies became mixed up with those wearing uniforms. That the officers got home at last on the right people is proved by the fact that these nightly murders became fewer and then practically ceased altogether.

It was into this scene of blood that we were hurled, and this was the condition which had become quite normal in the capital under the rule of the five-pointed Directorate. Its members were the most unmitigated failures that even poor distracted Russia had so far produced, and the people waited, hoping and longing, for their speedy removal. I was not at all surprised when, next morning, my liaison officer, Colonel Frank, returned from the Russian Headquarters in great perturbation and with great excitement informed me that Russia was doomed never to rise out of her troubles. I asked why. He answered that during the night some villains had arrested the Social Revolutionary members of the Directorate and Government, that no one at Headquarters knew the persons who had again upset the whole government of the country, and he had no doubt that the members of the late Government were already murdered. I took the necessary precautions for the safety of my command and awaited developments. I knew that the telegraph to the east was cut and that a *coup d'état* was in course of execution.

CHAPTER XI

AT 11 A.M. on November 18 I was officially informed that the Council of Ministers had met at 9 A.M., and were now in session, having met to consider the situation produced by the arrest of the Directorate. They had already asked Admiral Koltchak to accept supreme authority, that he had refused, but the Ministers had great hope that for the sake of Russia the admiral could be prevailed upon to take the burden of Government upon himself, as it appeared to be the only means of getting the country out of her desperate situation. The wildest rumours were in circulation : that my carriage would be attacked by bombs, that the British would at any time be obliged to fight for their lives. I told my informants that they need not worry about us; we were well able to take care of ourselves. They could not understand our indifference. The fact was that not a man or officer in my battalion had the slightest inkling of the position. Then the tune changed. Would I defend the Ministers who were still in session if they were attacked? My answer was that any political refugee who sought asylum in my lines would be protected, but he must give up every idea of again taking any part in

What Happened at Omsk

Russian affairs. "But what would you do if the Russian troops revolted and sought to murder those who had come into your lines. Would you give them up?" "Never!" "What if the Czech commanders made the demand?" "Still never; besides which the Czechs are too honourable ever to make a demand such as no soldier could accept." The last question was the most important of all, and was doubtless the kernel of the whole series, the others being mere camouflage.

The Czechs had just inaugurated their National Republican Government, and were naturally obsessed with the usual "Liberty, Equality, and Fraternity" business, and could not be expected to view the establishment of a Dictatorship within their sphere of operations with entire unconcern or without serious misgivings. The hostile attitude of the Russian branch of their National Council at Ekaterinburg and Chilliyabinsk, directly they heard of Koltchak's acceptance of the supreme authority, is proof of the danger which might evolve from that quarter.

The Council of Ministers, and perhaps Koltchak himself, were unable to take the final plunge until they had a thorough understanding of the British attitude. The position of the Czech forces at Omsk made it impossible for them to approach the place where the Ministers were in session without passing the British, and my machine guns commanded every avenue leading to or from the Russian Headquarters.

Things were now in such a state of tension that

for the safety of my command I informed both the Russian and Czech authorities that I should not allow bodies of troops or citizens either to approach or collect near my cantonment; that such approach or collection would be treated as hostile, and dealt with accordingly. That these arrangements gave the Ministers greater confidence to proceed with their policy I have no doubt. That was one of the inevitable consequences of the preparations for our own defence, but not the inspiration of their policy, which was entirely their own; but it did steady the situation.

I place these facts on record that those who are interested may be able to give them their proper order of value and importance. I afterwards learnt that more than one highly-placed official's wife had all preparations made for a rapid descent upon the Middlesex quarters.

About 2.30 P.M., November 18, I was informed that Admiral Koltchak had assumed absolute power under the title of " Supreme Governor," with a Council of Ministers who would be responsible to him for the proper performance of their duties; that he proposed to call on the French representative, Monsieur Renault, to present himself in the evening; that he would then call on me, as the senior British officer in Omsk, and in my case he would answer any questions I chose to put to him. He called, and it is as well to place here the report I made upon the subject at the time :

What Happened at Omsk

From Lieutenant-Colonel John Ward, M.P., C.M.G., Omsk, Siberia.

To G.O.C. China Command. Through B.M.M. H.Q.

Headquarters B.M.M., Vladivostok.

Sir,—For State reasons I deem it necessary to give the following information that it may be forwarded home to the proper authorities.

About 2.30 P.M. on November 18, 1918, my liaison officer (Colonel Frank, of the Russian Army) informed me that at a meeting of the Council of Ministers, just held, the Council had offered to place supreme sovereign power in the hands of Admiral Alexander Koltchak. The admiral had first refused to accept, but that such pressure had been applied to force him to accept that he had at last reluctantly consented.

Further, that Admiral Koltchak had assumed the title of " Supreme Governor of all Russia," and was calling upon the French Ambassador in the evening, after which he would call on me as the Senior British Officer holding official position in Omsk.

About 9 P.M. Admiral Koltchak called at my headquarters. The following gentlemen were present to receive him : Lieutenant-Colonel J. F. Neilson, Captain Stephani, Colonel R. Frank (Russian Army), and Mr. Frazer (*Times* correspondent). He wore the full dress of a Russian admiral.

The admiral, who speaks fair English, informed me of the circumstances and reasons for his assumption of supreme authority in all Russia.

With the " Die-Hards " in Siberia

An attempt had been made to combine all parties in the Government of the country to reduce it to a state of order, so that the people might be able to decide the future Government of Russia. The Council chosen by the Ufa Assembly had tried to work together for this purpose, but had failed. The final dissolution had been brought about by a proclamation issued by the Central Committee of the Social Revolutionary party, which was intended to produce in the new army the same conditions that had destroyed the old army. The proclamation had been signed by the Social Revolutionary President, Chernoff, and when it was proposed to take action against those who were destroying the discipline of the army, two Social Revolutionary members of the Council, Avkzentieff and Zenzinoff, could see nothing wrong in Chernoff's subversive propaganda. It later transpired that both were members of the Social Revolutionary Committee which had issued the literature in question, and refused to either leave the Social Revolutionary Committee or repudiate the anti-discipline propaganda of their friends.

This brought the new Government to a complete standstill, and, faced with absolute anarchy, the Council of Ministers had no alternative but to dissolve the old Directorate of Five and centre the supreme power in one person, to whom the Council of Ministers would be responsible for the administration of their several departments.

I answered that the reasons, coupled with my own knowledge, appeared to justify the action, but I had heard that the Social Revolutionary members

RUSSIAN HEADQUARTERS "STAFFKA" AT OMSK.

BRITISH STAFF AND C.O.'S WAGON.

What Happened at Omsk

of the Directorate and others had been arrested, and
that if this action supposed their execution it would
make the whole proceeding look like an attempt on
the part of the old army officers to destroy the
present arrangements in favour of a return to the
old régime. Further, if the people of England
thought this was the policy of the admiral and his
friends, they would not only lose the friendly
sympathy of the English people but also of America
and France.

Admiral Koltchak replied that at the moment he
did not know the whereabouts of the prisoners, but
he would make inquiries and inform me later. That
his sole object in burdening himself with the over-
whelming responsibilities of Supreme Governor of
Russia in this sad hour of her history was to prevent
the extremists on either side continuing the anarchy
which made the establishment of a free constitution
impossible. That if his action at any future time
was not in harmony with the establishment of free
political institutions as understood by the Democracy
of England, he would be convinced that he had
failed.

I thanked him for his good opinion of my
country, and called his attention to the letter of
His Majesty the King to President Wilson, received
at Omsk on November 14, 1918, in which the principles of democracy and freedom were exalted, and
warned him that the free peoples of the world would
resist any attempt to force the Russian people back
under a system of tyranny and despair.

Admiral Koltchak replied that he had read the

With the " Die-Hards " in Siberia

letter of His Majesty the King of England, and his one hope was that soon Russia might enjoy the blessing of equally free institutions.

Omsk, Siberia, *November*, 20, 1918.

From Lieutenant-Colonel John Ward, M.P., C.M.G., Omsk, Siberia.

To G.O.C. China Command.   Through B.M.M.

Headquarters B.M.M., Vladivostok.

Further Report on Political Crisis in Russia.

Following my report of the assumption by Admiral Koltchak of the supreme Governorship of Russia, I wish to add :

As I was unable to secure any official information relative to the whereabouts of the members of the Directorate who had been made prisoners during the night of November 17, I wrote to the Russian authorities (through Lieutenant-Colonel J. F. Neilson) on the night of the 18th requesting information upon the subject. On November 19, in the absence of information, I sent the following letter direct to Admiral Koltchak, the Supreme Governor :

OMSK, 19.11.18.   3 P.M.

From Colonel Ward.
To Admiral Koltchak.

After our interview last evening I sent you a note (through Lieutenant-Colonel J. F. Neilson) asking for information and some guarantee for the imprisoned members of the Council.

What Happened at Omsk

So far I have received no information upon the subject.

I have already told you that I am sure my country would look with grave concern upon any injury inflicted without proper trial upon these prisoners of State, and I should esteem it as a favour if you can supply me with information upon this subject.— Yours sincerely,

(Signed) JOHN WARD (Lt.-Col.).

Colonel Frank, my liaison officer, took the letter to Russian Headquarters, and on his return informed me that the admiral thanked me for my letter and that he was pleased to be able to allay my fears.

Three officers, named Lieutenant-Colonel Krasil-nikoff, Colonel Volkov, and Lieutenant-Colonel Katanaev, had presented themselves at Headquarters and reported that they took upon themselves the entire responsibility for the arrest of the members of the old Russian Government, that they had not injured them in any way, that they were prepared to hand their prisoners over to the authorities, together with several millions of roubles, believed to be loot, and papers which they had found in their possession. That the admiral had placed the prisoners under a strong guard of his own, and had placed the three officers under arrest to be tried by court-martial.

He further promised that no harm should come to them, and that he proposed to convey them out of the country at the earliest opportunity.

With the " Die-Hards " in Siberia

November 20.   1 P.M.

Admiral Koltchak, hearing that a supply guard of my battalion was returning to Vladivostok, has made request that I would allow the railway cars conveying the State prisoners to some unknown point on the Chinese frontier to be attached to my train for purposes of secrecy and additional safety. I have consented, and have strengthened the guard for this purpose.

Omsk, Siberia, *November*, 21, 1918.

[COPY.]

From Second-Lieutenant P. C. Cornish-Bowden, 25th Battalion Middlesex Regiment.

To The Adjutant, 25th Battalion Middlesex Regiment.

SIR,—I have the honour to report for the information of the Commanding Officer :

1. The train conveying the four Russian political exiles (Messrs. Avkzentieff, Argunoff, Rogovsky, and Zenzinoff) and the Russian guard, together with a detachment of British troops under my command, left Omsk about 2 A.M. on November 21, and arrived at Harbin on November 27. The journey was quiet. Most of the larger towns, where trouble was anticipated, were passed at night.

2. I have since been informed by the officer commanding the Russian guard that all traffic between Irkutsk and Chita was stopped by order of General Semianoff, and that the trains were

searched for the exiles after we had passed, but I have no evidence in support of this.

3. The exiles expressed the greatest possible gratitude for the presence of British troops, and said that they mistrusted their own Russian guard, though I saw nothing whatever at any time to lead me to believe their suspicions were well founded.

4. On arrival at Harbin the exiles strongly petitioned me to accompany the train to Chang-Chun, and the officers in charge of the Russian guard being quite willing, I decided to accompany the train to the Chinese-Manchurian frontier. We reached Chang-Chun about 2 A.M. on November 28, and the exiles left that place by themselves by train on the evening of the same day.

5. We reached Harbin again on the 29th inst., where I parted company with the Russian guard. We reached Vladivostok on the morning of December 2. I immediately reported to the O.C. Detachment, and I reported the before-mentioned facts verbally to General Knox.

6. The conduct of the N.C.O. and men of my detachment on the journey was very good, and no increase of sickness took place amongst them.—I have the honour to be, sir, your obedient servant,

(Signed) P. C. Cornish-Bowden
(Second-Lieutenant).

Vladivostok, Siberia, *December* 2, 1918.

I had already gained enough experience of revolutions to know that if I did not press my point

With the " Die-Hards " in Siberia

vigorously Avkzentieff and Co. were as dead as mutton. I also knew that my countrymen have a rooted dread of dictatorships, and that if Admiral Koltchak's assumption of power was either connected with or promoted by the execution of his opponents without trial, assistance or eventual recognition by the British Government would be made almost impossible. My own agents had discovered the place where the prisoners were detained, also that they were to be quietly bayoneted in the night, as shooting would attract attention. I was also certain that Koltchak knew nothing about this. The whole business was in the hands of an Officers' Revenge Society, a body who had sworn an oath to kill just the number of Bolshevik Revolutionaries as there had been officers murdered by Trotsky's and Avkzentieff's people. Both parties had similar combinations which left the marks of their foul deeds on the streets every night.

The state of affairs was such that only by a dictatorship could the most rudimentary order be maintained. I, a democrat, believing in government of the people by the people, thought I saw in the dictator the one hope of saving the remnants of Russian civilisation and culture. Words and names have never frightened me. If circumstances force on me a problem for solution, I never allow preconceived notions and ideas formed in the abstract, without the experience of the actual then existing facts, to warp my judgment in deciding the issue; and I am vain enough to believe that, had the same situation presented itself to Englishmen generally,

What Happened at Omsk

nine out of ten would act as I did. I merely
" carried on." The traditions of our race and
country did the rest.

Having, in my talk with the admiral and the
report I made, accepted his position of Supreme
Governor, I did not mean that he should be left to
fight his way unaided against the enemies who surrounded him. In other words, while outwardly
remaining neutral, I constantly made representations
and gave advice, when asked, about everything, both
internal and external; and here it may be interesting to our own people to know some of the problems
which confronted the Supreme Governor. The
Japanese question was the first. General Rosanoff
was Bolderoff's Chief of Staff, and it was important
to the Supreme Governor that he should get the
hang of outstanding matters and also make himself
fairly acquainted with the policy of the deposed
Directorate. He interviewed General Rosanoff and
the Staff generally, and discovered that after the fall
of Samara the Bolshevik army moved rapidly towards
Ufa, and the Directorate became so alarmed that
they demanded some definite policy from the Commander-in-Chief as to how he proposed to deal with
this menace. Bolderoff never thought of effectively
organising the new Russian army, but suggested
that things were so critical, and that England,
France, and America were so slow, that the only
alternative was to invite the Japanese to push their
army forward to the Urals. This was exactly what
Japan wanted, but the Japanese Staff demanded as
a *quid pro quo* to their advance to Ekaterinburg and

Chilliyabinsk that they should be placed in absolute possession of the railway and telegraph lines to those points. Bolderoff and the Directorate boggled at this for a time, but as the Bolsheviks began to get close to Ufa, and also concentrated an army of about one hundred thousand men for an offensive towards Ekaterinburg, the situation became so pressing that the Directorate gave way, and a few days before the *coup d'état* Bolderoff had sent word to the Japanese that their terms were accepted.

The Japanese had made all preparations to move when Koltchak took the reins in his own hands. He asked my advice. I advised him to say to the Japanese that the change of Government had also involved a change of policy, and that it would be inadvisable for the Japanese to advance beyond their position at Chita until the subject had been further discussed. They made him many tempting offers of help, both arms and money, but he refused them all, and they were unable to move him from the position he had taken up.

A subject that led to unfortunate bickerings between Admiral Koltchak and the French was the appointment by the Allied Council of Paris of General Ganin as the Commander of the Allied and Russian Forces in Siberia.

It is too important an item in the general failure of Allied policy to pass over without mention. From the very nature of the case the main Allied effort was the formation and organisation of a new Russian army. Our policy was not to prop Russia on her feet, but to enable her to stand by herself. Major-

What Happened at Omsk

General Knox had been sent out by the War Office to accomplish this purpose, and no more able or competent officer could have been appointed for the task.

General Knox had hardly begun to perform this duty when the French agents in Siberia became alarmed for their own position. Cables were dispatched to Europe pointing out the danger to French prestige which General Knox's mission entailed. If the English were to be made responsible for the reorganisation of the Russian Army, and were successful, this would tend to make New Russia rely more upon the English than the French, as had been the case hitherto; that it would be better to leave Russia without an army than have it organised under such influence. These senseless fears of our French friends found willing listeners in Paris. General Knox had already made some selections of officers and the business was well under way when a message from the Allied Council in Paris put an extinguisher on all his work. His orders were cancelled, and he was told to do nothing until a French commander had been appointed, whose name would be forwarded later.

By this uninformed Allied interference a well-thought-out scheme of army reorganisation was hung up for four of the most precious months to Russia. By the time General Ganin arrived the time for the project had passed and the whole business had been taken out of Allied hands.

The Russian situation at that time was such that four days' delay would have been fatal, and if nothing

had been done for four months we should have been
hunted out of the country.

Finding Allied jealousy so great as to render all
their efforts impotent, first General Bolderoff and
then his successor, the Supreme Governor, began to
organise armies on their own for the protection of
the people and their property. These armies were
ill-equipped and badly disciplined—not the kind of
armies which would have been raised had General
Knox's plans been allowed to develop—but they
performed their duty, they captured Perm, and had
increased to over 200,000 before General Ganin
appeared on the scene.

When General Ganin reported himself to the
Supreme Governor with the Allied Council's orders
to take over the command of the Allied and Russian
forces in Siberia, he was met with a blank refusal
from the Omsk Government.

I was consulted upon the question, and I am
therefore able to give the reasons for their objection.
The Omsk Government's position was a very simple
one: "Had General Knox or any other Allied
commander organised, paid, and equipped the new
Russian army he would have naturally controlled
it until such time as a Russian Government could
have been established strong enough to have taken
over the responsibility. The French would not
allow this to be done, and we ourselves therefore
undertook the duty. Having formed our own army
in our own country, it is an unheard of proposal that
we should be forced to place it under the command
of a non-Russian officer. It would be derogatory

What Happened at Omsk

to the influence and dignity of the Russian Government and lower the Government in the estimation of the people."

From this position they never retreated, but Allied bungling had landed General Ganin, who is himself an able and excellent officer, in a not very dignified position.

Bolderoff, as I have stated, was at the Ufa front when Koltchak assumed supreme power. He remained there in consultation with the Czech National Council and the members of the old Constituent Assembly for five or six days without a word as to his intentions. It was a critical position for Koltchak, who did not know what he was doing or intended to do. Hot-heads advised immediate action, but I suggested caution. The subject-matter of Bolderoff's conferences or whether he had any we do not know, but we do know this: General Dutoff, who commanded the Russian armies south of Ufa, had some proposals from Ufa put before him, and replied advising caution, as he had it on unimpeachable authority that the English were behind Admiral Koltchak. This statement, I was told, fell like a bombshell among the conspirators at Ufa, and soon after General Bolderoff returned to Omsk. There he interviewed Koltchak as Supreme Governor, and made satisfactory statement relative to his absence. He was offered a post, which he refused, stating that he wished to leave the country, as he did not believe that a dictatorship could help Russia out of her difficulties. His request was granted, and so ended a very different interview between these two men from that at Petropalovsk a few days before.

Some time after this the Japanese representative at Omsk made a request to be informed whether General Bolderoff had been forced to leave the country, or had left voluntarily. This was answered in a definite way in accordance with the facts. In the same note the Japanese also demanded to be informed whether the British Army had supplied the train and guard which had taken the exiled Social Revolutionary Members of the Directorate to Chang-Chun, on the Chinese frontier. This question was not answered quite so definitely, but the interest of the Japanese in these men shows how far the *coup d'état* had upset their plans relative to the occupation of the Urals.

The Supreme Governor issued definite orders to the different isolated sections of the Russian forces. All commanders obeyed these orders more or less except one, General Semianoff, whose headquarters were alongside that of the Japanese at Chita, from which he sent insolent refusals to recognise Koltchak's authority. Koltchak prepared to deal with this mutinous and buccaneering officer. The Japanese at once plainly informed the Omsk Government that General Semianoff was under their protection, and they would not allow the Russian Government to interfere with him.

Under Japanese protection this fellow continued to carry out indiscriminate executions and flogging of workment until the whole district became depopulated, and the Allies were forced to demand an

What Happened at Omsk

explanation from Japan for their extraordinary conduct. So fearful were they that their tool was about to be dealt with, that when the 1/9th Battalion of the Hampshire Territorial Regiment started from Vladivostok, the Japanese asked the Omsk Government whether these British troops were coming forward to attack General Semianoff. The answer we gave was that all movements of British troops were conducted by the British Military Mission, to whom they must apply for information. I never heard any more of their inquiries.

About this time a party of Cossacks, with a high officer at their head, called at the prison one night and produced to the governor an alleged order for the release of nine political prisoners. The [perhaps] unsuspecting governor handed his prisoners over; they were taken away, and next morning their friends found them shot. Someone ought to have been hanged, but Koltchak could find no one to hang. His Chief of Staff must have discovered some facts about the crime, but he refused to act. In fact, he did not acquaint the admiral about the crime until four days later when it had become public property. Koltchak was quite overcome, first with rage at the crime itself, and secondly at his impotence in being unable to prevent it. But Omsk went on the even tenor of its way : it is remarkable what horrors people can face without a tremor when they get used to them, as they must in revolutions.

CHAPTER XII

THE CAPTURE OF PERM : THE CZECHS RETIRE FROM THE FIGHTING

THE *coup d'état* had thrown the proposed Perm offensive completely into the background. The Czechs, under the influence of their Political Council, who had joined the Social Revolutionary Committee, and their leader Chernoff, retired to the rear. Each unit elected a committee and established a Soldiers' Council on the strictest Bolshevik plan, and ceased to be of further use either to the Russians or their own cause. The officers of the new Russian army became greatly concerned for the integrity of their own young troops with such a shocking example of lack of discipline before their eyes, and begged Admiral Koltchak to order these hostile political bodies out of Ekaterinburg. The admiral offered them a town in the rear where they might discuss politics to their hearts' content, without danger to his army. This, however, did not suit their plans, for their obvious object was to destroy the integrity of the new Russian army. Admiral Koltchak in desperation ordered the leaders to be arrested and the conspiracy to be broken up. General Gaida, though a Czech officer, put the admiral's order into effect, and handed the prisoners over to the Commander-in-Chief, General Surovey, at Chilliyabinsk. General

The Capture of Perm

Surovey, under pressure of the Czech Council and Chernoff's Committee, released the prisoners, and began to hunt the famous young General Gaida out of their hitherto equally famous army. To save himself from disgrace at the hands of his political enemies, the general resigned his commission in the Czech Army, and by joining the Russian Army was instantly re-established in his position as Commander of the Russian armies on the right. Thus fell the glorious Czech legions from their high pinnacle of fame, killed as all armies must be the moment they join in party strife.

From the point of view of purely Russian tactics, it was necessary to strike south from Ufa, with the object of effecting a junction with the Orenburg Cossacks under General Dutoff, and if possible linking up with the forces of General Denikin in South Russia. But no exact or reliable information could be secured as to the strength and equipment of Dutoff or Denikin.

On the other hand, it was known that an Anglo-American force had landed at Archangel, which it was presumed would be well supplied with winter equipment, and if once a junction could be effected with this force, a channel for European supplies could soon be opened. Every cartridge, gun, rifle, and article of clothing had now to be shipped almost round the world, and brought over about six thousand miles of more or less disorganised railway communication. Koltchak had men, but no means for making them into fighters unless supplied from outside. It was felt certain that if his armies could smash their way through to Perm, and hold a point somewhere between there and Vatka, the junction of the Archangel and Petrograd Railway, the slightest movement of the Archangel expedition would result in a combination which could and would move straight forward to Petrograd, and free north Russia from the Terrorists.

Originally I was to have operated in the centre with a detachment of the 25th Middlesex Battalion and four machine guns, and authority had been given for my part in the advance. The complete defection of the Czechs, however, threw the time-table out of joint, and not even the restless energy of the Supreme Governor could make up this loss for nearly four weeks. In the meantime the cold became so intense that the British contingent, being only B1 men, had to drop out. General Gaida, with his divisional generals, Galitzin, Pepelaieff, and Verzbitzky, pressed forward their preparations, and after a splendid series of movements captured Perm with 31,000 prisoners and an enormous booty of war material. The losses of the Russians were about 6,000 killed, of the Bolsheviks about 16,000. There were practically no wounded, for any man who sank in the snow was dead in an hour. Thus did the admiral consolidate the power that had been entrusted to him.

The Terrorists were completely demoralised, so that the army advanced to Glasoff, 80 miles east of Vatka and 60 miles south of Koltass. We were now only about 300 miles east of Petrograd, and there we waited for seven months for the Archangel move,

The Capture of Perm

which never came off. For some time the country was so absolutely clear of enemy forces that small parties of men passed unmolested from Glasoff to Archangel and from Archangel to Glasoff. Eventually the Terrorists got the correct measure of this Northern expedition, contained it with a slight screen, and concentrated huge forces to press us back over the Urals once more.

CHAPTER XIII

THE DECEMBER ROYALIST AND BOLSHEVIST CONSPIRACY

THE tenure of a dictator's office is very uncertain. He issues his orders, but if the army chiefs can escape from executing them they do so, on one pretext or another. The Russian character is most peculiar in this respect. It will obey one thing only—force. Patriotism and public spirit, as we know them, do not exist to any great extent. Every man looks at every order from the personal point of view—" How will this affect me? "—rarely, if ever, " How will it affect the country? "

It is remarkable how much Koltchak had already accomplished, but it seemed that his career might end at any moment, in spite of every precaution of his friends. Of these he had not many; no real dictator should expect to have any. No man will have many friends in Russia who puts personal questions second to the public welfare.

The preparations for the Perm offensive were well under way, when a dispatch came from General Dutoff, stating, " That in view of the pressure by our forces on their left the Bolshevik leaders had decided to, what they called, ' organise their enemies' rear.' That seventy of their best propagandist and most capable agents and officers had passed between his columns and were now distributed somewhere in our midst." All we could do was to wait, and see where this treacherous movement would show itself first.

The fact that Koltchak had declared for the calling of a National Assembly, elected by universal suffrage, to decide the future government of Russia, so soon as order was restored, had shattered completely the vision of the old army officers of a quick return to absolutism. His declaration against extremists on either side had driven Bolshevik and Tsarist into practically one camp. He was well known as a student of English customs and institutions and a pre-revolution advocate of constitutionalism. The Tsarist section hoped that his assumption of supreme authority was proof that he had discarded his democratic principles, but gradually his official declarations to the representative of the British Government leaked out and spread consternation in the ranks of both sections of the Absolutists. The Bolshevik leaders have never made any bones about their fear and dread of democracy as understood in England, and have declared they would prefer a return to the old régime rather than have a Constitution like that of England or America forced upon them. Hence there is no real difference of principle between the Bolshevik and the supporters of the old régime, only a difference as to who should wield the power. For the moment they let this minor point slip into the background, and combined for the destruction of the man who was the enemy of both.

About midnight, December 23, Russian Headquarters gave me the alarm. Shots were being fired in all directions, and a spent bullet struck my carriage while I was getting into my clothes. Horsemen in little groups were surrounding the Staffka without much sign of order. Having inspected my battalion at their emergency quarters, I called for a personal guard to escort me to Headquarters. I regret there was no impressionist artist with us to record the weird procession my guard made. When sheepskin coats were provided for my men for use in a cold, snow-bound country, it is a real English touch that they should have been black in colour, making my men a perfect target both night and day. Their fur caps were a dark brown of the well-known Nansen type, the half-moon peak making the head of the wearer a good mark at midnight up to 300 yards. The cap is pointed, and has much the appearance at night of a small mitre. What with huge fur boots, black pointed caps, and long black coats, there was nothing to indicate the British Tommy in the line of black monks that moved silently forward over the frozen snow. The temperature was such that as the slight wind brought the water to one's eyes the drops froze to hard white spots of ice at the corners. Breath from the nostrils froze before it could leave the nose, and from each nostril hung icicles, in some cases 2 inches long, which again froze to the moustache. The eyebrows and eyelashes and the protruding fur edge which enclosed the faces of the men carried a wonderful display of hoar frost, and gave the appearance of white lace frills, such as are seen on " granny's " caps.

Royalist and Bolshevist Conspiracy

As we entered the Russian Headquarters, which were crowded with more or less excited officers and men, my guard lined up on each side of the vestibule, and without a word proceeded to unsling rifles and fix bayonets. The Russians, who were even now debating on which side they were going to slide down, looked at my soldier monks, and at once themselves fell into line. There was no longer any hesitation. "Anglisky soldats" were in possession of Russian Headquarters, and the reputation of English soldiers in emergencies like this is known all over the world. I interviewed the Chief-of-Staff, General Lebediff, as to his orders for suppressing the revolters and went downstairs to find the vestibule empty except for my " monks." No one who was not there could believe the absolute transformation that the mere presence of a few English soldiers had on this critical situation. In revolutions every rule and safeguard of society is uprooted; the people feel as in an earthquake, nothing is secure, everyone doubts his neighbour. If those who are prepared to support authority can only discover at the right moment one little group round whom they can rally, and who they know will think nothing of death in performance of duty, the danger is over at once. Hesitancy disappears, and the normal is instantly produced. We filed out to find the infantry in their ranks, and the horsemen mounted in line, under their officers, awaiting orders.

I proceeded through the town to the residence of the Supreme Governor. On our way we passed parties of soldiers and Cossacks hurrying to their posts, who eyed us suspiciously, but on seeing me at

With the "Die-Hards" in Siberia

the head in the uniform of a British officer, ejaculated loudly to their command the magic word "Anglisky," until like a talisman the word passed from sentry to sentry and street to street, and "Anglisky" became the password which held the whole town for law and order. We passed towards the admiral's house without challenge until the Cossack and Serbian guard at the actual extrance called us to halt pending the governor's orders. The order soon came for us to enter. The admiral was ill, very ill with inflammation of the lungs, but as brave as ever. My "monks" lined up in the vestibule in the same manner as at Headquarters, and even the personal Serbian guard had to make way for these queer-looking visitors. I got the information required. The revolt was very serious, but I was able to inform the admiral that effective measures had now been taken to provide for all eventualities. I begged leave to depart, which was granted, but not before my men had been given food and a taste of Russian vodka, which appears to be the only effective antidote to the cold of a real Siberian winter. I returned, to find that the fact that the English soldiers were out was known in every house in Omsk, and numerous requests from the highest to the lowest for protection had been received on the telephone. I give no names, but the fact shows what a remarkable influence the presence of a few British soldiers had in steadying the situation.

My orders were to take no part in the internal affairs of Russia, but it is the duty of every commanding officer to take all possible means to protect

Royalist and Bolshevist Conspiracy

his command. If I had remained in my quarters and made no sign until these Royalist and Bolshevik enemies had obtained possession of the town, I should have presented a dainty morsel which they could have masticated at leisure. I had to show my hand early enough to make sure it did not go against me. It turned out that I marched from my barracks just when news had been brought of the mutiny, under Royalist and Bolshevik leadership, of two companies of the 8th Regiment of the new Russian army. A body of Bolsheviks at Koulomsino, on the other side of the river, had taken up arms and were bent on the destruction of the bridge over the Irtish, which formed the means of communication with the armoured trains of H.M.S. *Suffolk*, and our naval detachments at Ufa. The Czechs (our Allies), who had the same orders as myself, on learning that the Tsarists were also in the conspiracy, frustrated this scheme by instantly moving forward a company for the protection of the bridge, which arrived just in the nick of time. Had we acted strictly to orders, Heaven only knows what the result would have been. British and Czech both had to act on our own judgment, and while, technically, we disobeyed orders, we fulfilled the policy of each country and protected our commands.

It cost nearly a thousand lives to restore order, but the lawless elements, top and bottom, were taught a lesson they are not likely to forget. This happened in the middle of the Perm offensive. It did nothing to assist the Bolshevik cause, but it did much to embitter the struggle.

CHAPTER XIV

A BOMBSHELL FROM PARIS AND THE EFFECT

THE foregoing incidents gave place to more personal matters. About December 28 the Staff of the Canadian contingent under Lieutenant-Colonel Morrisy arrived, and, as one might expect, revolutionary plans in connection with the distribution of my battalion, and other matters, were instantly proposed. Some of them were actually carried out, with the result that a strained feeling became manifest in the British camp at Omsk, which caused me to propose to Brigadier-General Elmsley that my headquarters should be transferred to Vladivostok. Luckily the arrival of the 1/9th Hampshire Territorial Battalion on January 5, 1919, under the Command of Lieutenant-Colonel Johnson, led to an improved condition of things all round us. This officer gripped the situation at once, and took such steps, in conjunction with the High Commissioner, Sir Charles Eliot, that I was prevailed upon to withdraw my request for the removal of my headquarters. Colonel Johnson was a great accession of strength to those who held the purely English point of view, and his battalion, recruited as it was from my home county, helped to make all our relations wonderfully cordial. General Elmsley replied later refusing my request, so that everything fitted in just right.

A Bombshell from Paris and the Effect

On January 8 a parade was called to present General Stephanik with the Legion of Honour and Major-General Knox, the Chief of the British Military Mission, and myself with the Croix de Guerre. It was a real Siberian day, " 62 below," and in five minutes ten men had frost-bitten ears. General Ganin, the French Commander-in-Chief of the Allied forces, made the presentations on behalf of the French Republic, uttering a few words to each recipient. I received the hearty congratulations of all our friends, which kept me warm the whole day. I thanked Colonel Pichon, who took over from me the command of the Ussurie front, and with whom I acted for some time, for this great honour. I felt sure that my decoration was the result of his reports upon myself while acting together under very awkward circumstances.

Towards the middle of January the British High Commissioner conveyed to Admiral Koltchak an extremely sympathetic message from the British Government. The French High Commissioner followed next day with a similar message from the French Government, except that it distinctly referred to the possibility of help and recognition. The Allied representatives felt more happy and secure as a result of these felicitations than they had done for some time, and the Russian authorities began to feel it possible to press on with the work of " resurrection." A new page in the history of a great recovery had been added to Russian records. Exactly four days later a wireless message came through from Paris to say that the Allied Council had declared that it could give no help or recognise either side; that the different parties and Governments existing in Russia must bring about an armistice, and send representatives to the Turkish "Isle of Dogs," near Constantinople, and arrange a compromise with each other. In other words, that the Bolsheviks were to be recognised as legitimate belligerents, with whom it was quite possible to shake hands and sit down to draw up an agreement as to the proper method of conducting a policy of rapine, robbery, and murder. Needless to say, every Britisher was disgusted, and every genuine Russian patriot simply amazed. At one swoop down went all our hopes! We were crushed as much or more than the Russians, because we had the honour of our countries to defend, and defence seemed impossible.

A sudden reaction against the European Allies set in at once, and became so violent that a Russian gentleman made an abusive speech to the Allied officers as they sipped tea in a well-known restaurant, and the public refused to allow the guard which was called to arrest him to carry out the order. This feeling was undoubtedly exploited by the Japanese for their own purposes.

A very tense condition of affairs existed, when on January 31 I asked for a special interview with Admiral Koltchak that I might introduce my colleague and comrade, Colonel Johnson, and talk over the situation. The admiral was out walking by the river, quite unattended, but in full view of the guard at his residence near the river bank. It was his first walk since his illness, and he looked quite recovered.

A Bombshell from Paris and the Effect

The talk naturally veered round to the Allied declaration in favour of the Bolsheviks and the situation it had created in Omsk. The admiral's attitude was quite simple. " We can talk and make compact with every party and Government in the different districts of Russia, but to compromise with Bolshevism, or shake the hand, or sit down and treat as equals the men who are outraging and murdering the Russian people—never! No decent Allied Government acquainted with the facts would ever expect it."

I asked him to consider the question as in no way decided by the Paris message, that I felt sure there must be some points connected with the decision that required further elucidation. " Yes ! " said the admiral. " There must be some facts with which we are not acquainted, for while the British Government advise an arrangement with the Bolsheviks they continue to furnish me with generous supplies for the Russian Army." I left quite satisfied that he still retained his faith in the friendship of England.

There was one queer point which needs to be placed on record. Admiral Koltchak observed that the Japanese were still causing him much trouble. They had been unable to approach him personally but had been " getting at " his officers, whose business caused them to make frequent visits to the Ural front. They made statements to the effect that the only state which was in a position to help Russia was Japan. The other armies were war-weary and clamouring for demobilisation and therefore unwilling to fight the Bolsheviks. If Admiral Koltchak was compelled to make a reasonable arrangement with

With the "Die-Hards" in Siberia

Japan, their army would guarantee to liquidate the Bolshevik forces in two months and establish a monarchy satisfactory to the Russian officers. This propaganda had reached the front, and had been referred to as assuming very serious importance by his front-line generals in their dispatches. To counteract this pernicious influence, he was proposing to visit the front himself to point out the impossibility of Japan, as one of the Entente Allies, being able herself to execute such a programme. I asked him how this propaganda began and who engineered it. He answered: "General Muto and a staff of twenty-six officers and intelligence assistants are working hard here in Omsk to influence Russian opinion in their direction." Finally the Supreme Governor said, "I make no complaint against these very excellent Japanese officers, they are only carrying out the orders of their political and military chiefs, but it makes my work of restoring order much more difficult."

There were other little rifts within the lute. The Russian officers are Royalist almost to a man, and will remain so, for they are all most childlike in their adherence to this principle. Some gossip informs one of them that Prince Kuropotkin is still alive and has been seen on the Russian frontier. "Oh!" he exclaims. "Then the admiral will be handing over his power to Kuropotkin directly he hears the prince is alive!" Next day he may be told that the prince is not a soldier and his enthusiasm at once oozes out of his finger tips. The next day some British supplies arrive, and then he is all for reliance upon the

A Bombshell from Paris and the Effect

Allies. A few days later, the Government not having been recognised by the Powers according to his wish, he curses the Powers and becomes morose. The day following he hears in a restaurant that Demitri-Pavlovitch is hiding as a peasant in Siberia, and he is immediately in about the same ecstatic condition as the shepherds who beheld the Star over Bethlehem. Every possible—or impossible—person under the sun becomes to him a potential saviour of his country; never does he think how he and his comrades themselves might save her. The Russian officer, indeed, is "just a great, big, brave, lovable baby, and nothing else." " Gulliver's Travels " ought to have an immense circulation should it ever be translated into the Russian language. The " Arabian Nights " appears as an unimaginative narrative of humdrum events compared with the stories in current circulation in Omsk and Siberia generally.

The two following extracts from my diary record incidents which occurred at this time.

"February 1, 1919. Last night three Bolshevik conspirators entered the officers' quarters of the 1st and 2nd Siberian Regiment disguised as Russian soldiers. The first intimation outside that anything was wrong was rapid revolver shots inside. The sentry captured one of the imitation soldiers as he tried to escape from the building. In less than two minutes the conspirators had shot five officers, two of whom were mortally wounded in the stomach. One conspirator was shot dead, one was captured, one got away. The knout was applied to the prisoner, and at the hundredth stroke he gave the whole conspiracy

With the " Die-Hards" in Siberia

away. Over fifty arrests followed his confession, with the result that all is again quiet in Omsk."

" February 3, 1919. Lieutenant Munro has just arrived at Omsk from Vladivostok with comforts from the ladies at Shanghai, Hong-Kong and Singapore. Words fail to describe the feelings of both officers and men as they received these tokens of love and remembrance from their own countrywomen in this cold inhospitable climate. It is a beautiful feeling, and though the actual work performed is the effort of a few, the whole sex receives a crude sort of deification from these womanly acts. The way one of the commonest Tommies looked at a small wash-flannel that had evidently been hemmed by hands unused to work of any description, and asked me if I would give the lady his thanks, would have gone to the heart of the fair but unknown worker could she have witnessed it.

" I heard news of general insubordination among the Canadian troops that had just arrived at Vladivostok. If all the information received could be relied upon, the sooner they were shipped back to Canada the better. There is enough anarchy here now without the British Government dumping more upon us. I can see that it is a great mistake to mix Canadians and British troops in one Brigade. Naturally, British soldiers carry out orders ; if other troops do not, then the British troops have to do all the work. The situation produced is that the highest paid soldier does no work and the lowest paid all the work. It soon percolates to the slowest Sussex brain that discipline does not pay. Nothing but the wonderful sense of order

A Bombshell from Paris and the Effect

in the make-up of the average Englishman has prevented us from becoming an Anglo-Canadian rabble, dangerous to Bolshevik and Russian alike. I am told that Brigadier Pickford had done his best to maintain order and discipline in his ranks; that he had been compelled to make very awkward promises to his troops which having been made had to be fulfilled. In all the circumstances it was generally agreed that the proper thing to have done was to send the Canadians home to their farms, and leave the few Britishers who were there to carry on. We had established excellent relations with the Russians which it would have been a thousand pities to spoil.''

CHAPTER XV

WHILE the loyal Russian officers were being murdered in their beds, other events not less important were happening. When Admiral Koltchak assumed supreme authority the Directorate was surrounded by a party of Royalist officers as turbulent and lawless as Trotsky himself. Private code messages passed between these officers as freely as if they already had the power in their own hands. The first intimation that Koltchak had of these conspiracies was a code message from General Evanoff Renoff to General Beloff, General Bolderoff's Chief of Staff, which unfolded many of the aspirations of these men, and showed their objects to be exclusively personal. I read these messages with great interest, as they gave me an excellent insight into the mainsprings of the revolution and incidentally into the character of the average Russian officer. General Antonovsky, of the old Russian Military Academy, who also assisted in the drafting of the Brest-Litovsk Treaty with the Germans, was a participant in the scheme, and was within an ace of becoming the admiral's Chief of Staff. Everything was working splendidly, when the cipher message from Renoff opened the ball. Beloff was sent to the east, and Antonovsky to the south, and the Absolutists became broken up.

More Intrigues

On February 1 my liaison officer informed me that as he waited in the corridor of headquarters, General Beloff came out of General Lebediff's room. A little later General Antonovsky came out of another room, and then these two were suddenly joined by a certain Cossack general of a very truculent type. I knew that this boded badly for order, and I warned Koltchak's young aide-de-camp. Shortly after it was reported to me that an attempt had been made to exchange a sham guard for the real one at the Supreme Governor's residence. That night I held our direct wire from Colonel Johnson to my ear till 12.30 A.M., and found that it was tapped by Russian Headquarters. General Knox had got to know things, and took certain action, with the result that I sent my officer to Russian Headquarters with instructions to inform General Lebediff we were anxious for the Supreme Governor's safety; that if any harm was contemplated against him we should hold him responsible unless he made us acquainted with the danger in time to avert it; further, that if the Absolutist officers thought they could murder Admiral Koltchak and proclaim an absolute Monarchy without the sanction of the people of Russia they were mistaken; that whoever, whether high or low, attempted to destroy the present Government and throw Russia back into violence and anarchy would be treated as enemies by the British soldiers. General Lebediff answered that he knew of no special danger threatening Admiral Koltchak at the moment, but he thanked Colonel Ward for his offer to help protect the Government in case of necessity.

With the " Die-Hards " in Siberia

The conspirators broke up at once, but the cunningest of the lot remained to weave again by social strategy the continuous web of Russian disorder. We knew that there were elements at work for a counter-revolution quite uncontrolled by, but acting with, the cognisance of officials of the Koltchak Administration. In revolutions sudden outbursts on the part of even a small party may soon jeopardise the whole organisation of State. Colonel Johnson and myself agreed that it was necessary to concentrate our forces, and in approaching the Russian authorities on this subject, we added further to the demoralisation of those who were in the conspiracy. We protested that it was our own safety that we had in view, but the conspirators did not believe us. I knew that the admiral's train had been for some days standing ready to take him to the front. On February 3 Omsk was informed that the important Japanese Mission (previously referred to) had started from Irkutsk on the last stage of its journey to the Supreme Governor. The governor's aide-de-camp informed me at the same time that the admiral was starting for the front at 5 P.M. on February 7.

General Knox was anxious that there should be no evidence of weakening in our support of the Omsk Government, as in case of disorder our position was by no means secure. After consultation it was decided to offer the admiral a personal guard for his journey, to consist of fifty men and one officer from the Hampshire Regiment. This was accepted and referred to the Chief of Staff for confirmation. It was then reported to General Ganin and the French

More Intrigues

Staff. They at once protested that to have a purely English guard would lower French prestige in the eyes of the Russians. They quite agreed that there ought to be a guard, but it must be half English and half French, and to this we at once agreed. We therefore reduced our number to twenty-five. Then, however, the French Staff pointed out that they had no troops in Omsk, and they could not leave the Staff without a cook. The greatest number of orderlies they could spare was nine, so it was suggested that the guard should consist of forty-one English and nine French soldiers. This took the negotiators' breath away entirely; the first proposal was destructive of French prestige, the second was enough to destroy France altogether! Really France is much too beautiful and gallant a country to have this sort of stuff put forward on her behalf, but there it was. So the admiral's guard consisted of nine soldiers with one officer of each nationality—twenty all told.

One point we did get home on. At the time appointed for the admiral's departure, an English guard of honour miraculously appeared on the scene, together with Russian and Czech guards. There *could* be no French—yet French prestige continued to stand just as high as ever it did. I give these facts in the most friendly spirit, but with a hope that English officers will always understand that, however much we smile at the peculiar gyrations of the word " prestige " as understood by our Continental neighbours, it is very real to them, and strange exhibitions of it are seen on occasions.

The Supreme Governor had arrived and shaken

hands with the Russian, English and Czech representatives, including Sir Charles Eliot, the British
High Commissioner, and General Bowes, the Chief
of the British Military Mission to the Czecho-Slovaks.
The French representative was late. When the ceremonial was nearly complete, a French officer (not
above the rank of captain) elbowed his way to the
front and vigorously brushed aside the British High
Commissioner and general, and stood with his back
towards them as though they were mere outside
spectators who had no business there. The same
evening the incident was being discussed amongst a
group of Russian and English officers, when a Russian
officer of the highest position observed, "You English have the queerest notion of national prestige of
all the countries I have been so far acquainted with.
Any ordinary Russian, Kirghis, Tartar, or Mongolian officer seeing a French captain brush aside the
representatives and generals of another state would
instantly decide that he only did so not because of
want of politeness, which one-half the world does not
understand, but because the nation to which he
belongs was so great and powerful there was no need
to be deferential to any of the others, and especially
so to the state whose representatives allowed themselves to be so easily brushed aside."

We had many conferences upon the condition
of the Russian workman, and whether it was possible
for the Allies to do anything to help them. British
officers were making desperate efforts to organise and
equip forces capable of dealing a death-blow to the
Bolsheviks in the early spring. General Knox worked

More Intrigues

like a Trojan, and gave more inspiration to the Russian Government than all the other Allied representatives put together. In fact, without his sagacity and determination we should have been better employed at home. He travelled from " Vlady " to Omsk, from Omsk to " Vlady," as though the 5,000-mile journey was just a run from London to Birmingham. His great strength was that he made up his mind on a certain course, and stuck to it, while everyone around him could never decide upon anything for long. If you want anything done, don't have Allies. Allies are all right when a powerful enemy is striking you or them; it is then quite simple; mere self-preservation is sufficient to hold you together for common protection. Let the danger pass, let the roar of conflict recede in the distance, and Allies become impotent for any purpose except spying on each other and obstructing the work in hand. There was no evidence that anyone, except the English, was doing anything to smooth the way for the new Russian Government, but by sheer energy General Knox had brought together personnel and stores sufficient to justify belief in the early success of his plans. Then there suddenly arose another sinister figure which threatened to upset all our calculations—namely, a well-timed revolt of the railway workmen, calculated to cripple our communications and make the movement of troops and supplies impossible.

CHAPTER XVI

RUSSIAN LABOUR

GENERAL DUTOFF, as I have previously recorded, had informed us that Bolshevist agitators had passed through our lines on this treacherous mission, and for months nothing had been heard of these emissaries of mischief. Now that we were approaching the critical point of the 1919 operations rumblings of an unmistakable character were heard in all directions. The necessary military measures had been taken, but in our English eyes suppression was not enough. We have learnt in our country that the workmen are the backbone of the State, and that when labour is badly paid the heart of the State is diseased. Russia has no ideas about labour at all. The autocracy never gave it a moment's consideration. The last Tsar's idea of labour reform was to abolish good vodka, and he lost his life. The officer class, that forms so large a proportion of Russian life, never gave the subject five minutes' consideration. There is not a single general labour law upon the statute book of Russia, and the horror of it is that those who have hitherto pretended to lead the Russian workman refuse to demand laws to protect their labour. They believe that " law " is the last thing that a workman robbed of the most elemental rights should think about; that the only way for a workman to obtain rights

Russian Labour

is to abolish all "law." And this they have done
with a vengeance! The professional Russian labour
leader is an anarchist and nothing else, and in
Bolshevism he has given a glimpse of his policy in
practice.

This, then, was the problem with which we had
to deal, and with only a few weeks at our disposal.
To the Russian workman it was a social question; to
us it was both social and military. Finally, General
Knox asked me to undertake a pacific propaganda
along the railway to see if it were possible to persuade
the workmen to keep at work and give the best service
possible to their country to secure the restoration of
order. I came to the conclusion that if anything
could be done to give a more staple and practical
outlook to the Russian labour mind it was well worth
trying to accomplish it.

At the outset I was faced with the difficulty of
not being in a position to offer anything definite to
the workmen in return for their willingness to assist
the combatant branch of the Russian service in its
new crusade against anarchy. With nothing to offer
it seemed hopeless to ask for so much. The only man
who could pledge the Government was the Supreme
Governor himself, so I wrote to him as follows:

[COPY.] OMSK, SIBERIA.
4th February, 1919.

To His High Excellency, ADMIRAL KOLTCHAK,
Supreme Governor.

SIR,—I have been requested by Major-General Knox,
Chief of the British Military Mission, Siberia, to undertake a tour of the railway works along the Siberian

With the "Die-Hards" in Siberia

Railway to address the workmen, and appeal to them as a British Labour representative to give their best service to the Russian State during the present and coming military operations, and to join no strike movement, or do anything to hamper the transport of men and supplies until the military operations against the enemy are completed.

I have pointed out to General Knox that, while I am quite willing to undertake this mission to the railway workmen, I fear it will be quite useless unless I can promise, on behalf of the Russian Government, some improvement in their condition.

1. For instance, I am informed that some of the railway and other Government workmen have not received any wages upon which to keep themselves and their families, for in some cases many weeks, and in other cases months. If this is true, it is impossible to expect workmen to be satisfied, and the wonder would be that they agree to work as well as they do.

It would be necessary for me to be able to promise that such things would be rectified, and wages paid regularly in future.

2. There are many things absent in Russia which industrial communities like England find necessary elements for industrial peace. I admit that very little constructional reform work can be executed during the present disturbed condition of the country, but it would help immensely if I could tell the workmen that I had the authority of the Russian Government that directly order had been restored, laws for the protection and help of the Russian workmen and their organisations, on the lines of those already working so effectively in England, would be adopted by the Russian Government.

Russian Labour

If I could get something definite from Your High Excellency upon these points, I believe it would do much to help in the work for the pacification of the labouring classes of Russia, and greatly strengthen Your Excellency's hold upon the hearts of the Russian people.

(Signed) JOHN WARD.

(Lt.-Colonel, M.P., C.M.G., Commanding 25th Bn. Middlesex Regiment.)

[COPY.]   OMSK.
February 5th, 1919.

SIR,—In reply to your letter of February 4th, I wish to inform you that I have learned with the greatest satisfaction that you are willing to undertake the important mission of addressing the workmen of our railways and calling them to give their best service to the cause of Russia in this crucial moment of our national existence.

The two questions which you have raised in your letter should not be left without a prompt answer, and I therefore would like to bring to your knowledge the following :—

1. The imperative necessity of orderly and regular payment of wages to the workmen has been the object of my personal anxiety, and pressing measures in that direction have been urged by the Government. The railways being considered by us just as important as the army, you will understand that everything in its power will be done by our Government to help the threatening situation in that respect.

2. As for the second question which you have mentioned in your letter, I venture to assure you that the Government has already stated in its official programme that the workmen will find protection and help in the

With the "Die-Hards" in Siberia

laws which shall be enforced and have to secure their organisation on lines similar to those of democratic states in Europe. The Government has actually a special Department of Labour which is preparing the future legislation on this question, following the general course of constructive reform work which I hope to be able to pursue with all the energy and vigour that the military situation will permit.

I take this opportunity to renew the expression of my profound appreciation of the interest you take in our situation and of the valuable assistance you so generously offer in this most important matter of pacification of the labouring classes in Russia.

Yours sincerely,

(Signed)   A. KOLTCHAK.

Lt.-Colonel JOHN WARD, M.P., C.M.G.,
Commanding 25th Bn. Middlesex Regiment.

This is believed to be the first correspondence ever conducted by the head of any Russian Government upon a purely labour subject. It shows that in supporting Admiral Koltchak we had at least this fact to recommend our policy : that he was a democrat, and anxious that his country should be in labour matters amongst the first flight of nations.

The question now to be solved was : What attitude would the anarchist adopt to this new evangelism?

I was ready to start on my journey when there began such a blizzard as is occasionally described in the literature of Polar exploration. For forty-eight hours from the south came a furious gale. It was not too cold, only about twenty degrees of actual frost, but with the wind came blinding snow—not

Russian Labour

snow such as we see in England, but fine snow, like white dust. It beat on your face, found its way between the flaps of your head-covers, where it thawed and ran down your neck and chest and saturated your underwear. It smashed straight on to your eyeballs, and froze in cakes to your eyelashes and cheeks, so that in five or ten minutes you were blind and unable to find your way or move in any direction. All sentries had to be withdrawn and sent to the nearest shelter, for it was impossible to locate onself or see a building till you blundered up against it. A note in my diary records that " a guard of eighteen Russians and one officer walked away from their post and have not been seen since, and six days have passed." Roofs were torn off the houses, and the strongest buildings rocked in a most alarming manner. The snow piled itself up against the houses till it covered the windows on the ground floors and half-way up those of the second. This southern gale took twenty-four hours in which to blow itself out, and a four days' calm followed, during which the snow was cleared from the railway and traffic resumed. The next startler was a message from Irkutsk stating that a terrific gale was breaking down from the north—a recoil from the one just described—accompanied with sixty degrees of actual frost, making it impossible to live out of doors. This storm struck Omsk on February 20, and no words can describe the complete obliteration of man and all his works accomplished by such a gale. Nothing can live in the intense cold created by such a wind. Hence movement and life cease, and King Frost has the whole field to himself. In a few hours the earth is levelled; all the indications remaining of the ordinary log dwellings are a few snow-banks with a row of dark posts from which smoke is emitted, showing that there are human habitations underneath. By February 22 this storm had worked itself out and we were able to proceed.

The influence of the Koltchak Government could be seen in the orderly management of affairs connected with the railway and supplies generally. Not till we reached Kamergah could we observe any sign that there still remained unextinguished embers of the social inferno through which the country had passed. At this point the line was guarded by a strong detachment of troops quartered in trucks on the siding. The officer in command informed me that an attack by revolters had been made on the line at this point, who had held up the traffic for some hours, but had been driven off before any permanent injury was accomplished. The revolters did not wait after the attack, but set fire to the station and departed. He suggested that it might be as well to be ready for sniping, and for worse things, should accident force the train to come to a standstill between here and Krasnoyarsk. We arrived at the latter place, however, without incident on February 25.

Krasnoyarsk is a fairly large town on the River Yenesei. The fine bridge over the river is the point to which the eyes of the revolters are constantly directed. The garrison was composed of one company of the 25th Middlesex Regiment, an Italian

Russian Labour

battalion recently formed from amongst the Italian prisoners of war and armed by the British, about four hundred Cossacks, and a company of Czechs belonging to the 10th Regiment, who arrived that morning. There were numbers of Bolsheviks inhabiting an elevated part of the town. These met on the old Russian New Year's Day and passed a resolution that it was necessary to execute all army officers wherever they might be found isolated from their comrades. The army chiefs replied by ordering all guns to be trained on the Bolshevik part of the town and one round of shell from each of the eight guns to be planted in the Bolshevik quarters for every officer murdered. No officers had been murdered up to that time. A party of Serbians who had been armed to assist in protecting the inhabitants were caught selling arms and ammunition to the Bolsheviks; they were surrounded in the middle of the night and disarmed, one Cossack being killed. The 25th were "standing to" during this operation in case their assistance was required.

We started for Irkutsk on the 25th, having been warned that the road to Kansk was practically dominated by the revolters. About 8 P.M. we arrived at the headquarters of General Affinasiaff, who came into my car and gave a minute description of the situation. The enemy forces numbered about 8,000, and those of the Russian Government about 3,000. For about one hundred versts the Russian forces, in small detachments, were allowing themselves to be pinned to the railway.

It was very interesting to hear a clear statement

With the " Die-Hards " in Siberia

as to the cause of the revolt and to find that the chief point of the grievances set forth in the revolters' own proclamations. In great part these opponents of the Government consist of rich peasants, who already possessing land which in many cases was equal in extent to the County of Rutland, had in 1917, under the order of Lenin and Trotsky, taken forcible possession of the furniture, horses, farmhouses, carts, carriages, land, etc., of the big landholders, who with their families had been massacred by these same rich peasants.

The next important element among the revolters were the escaped prisoners of the old régime, who, being released by the Bolsheviks, had taken to the forest to avoid recapture—probably the wildest and most savage set of men in the world. They were illicitly fed and protected by the aforementioned wealthy peasants with a view, firstly, to buy off their hostility to themselves, and, secondly, to secure their help to resist the civil officers of the new Government who were appointed to inquire into the methods by which these wealthy peasants became possessed of their dead neighbours' lands and properties; thirdly, to enable these wealthy peasants to resist the payment of taxes, not only those that were in arrears, but any that would become due in the future. This was the point dealt with in their proclamation, wherein it was stated that inasmuch as it was the people who lived in the towns that forced the revolution, therefore it was unjust to ask the peasants to pay for the damage done by those in the towns; further, that it was the people in the

Russian Labour

towns who kept on fighting one another, and until they had finished their quarrelling the peasants would not pay any taxes or do anything to help the Government; fourthly, this unholy partnership enabled the wealthy peasants to resist the mobilisation ordered by the Koltchak Government for the same reasons.

As I have already pointed out, every minor Government and general, including General Denikin, made haste to show their submission to Omsk when Admiral Koltchak assumed authority, the only exception being Colonel Semianoff. He, it was known, was accepting a regular subsidy from the Japanese to enable them to resist the extension of the admiral's power towards Vladivostok, and it was under their instructions and protection Semianoff refused to recognise the authority of the Omsk Government and issued insolent manifestos against the Supreme Governor. The peasants inhabiting the western side of the Baikal seized upon this fact and said in their proclamations that inasmuch as Colonel Semianoff had refused to allow Koltchak's orders to operate on the east side, and was supported therein by one of the Allies, there was every reason why they should do the same on the west side of the lake. It shows what a tremendous influence Japan had either to create order or to make order impossible. She and Semianoff between them provided these revolters with just the argument they needed. By so acting Japan created and extended the area of anarchy and made the task of her Allies and Koltchak more difficult than it might otherwise have been.

With the " Die-Hards" in Siberia

This may not be a very logical position for the peasants to have taken up, but anyone who knows anything about Russia will see that it fitted their psychology to a fraction. These people are more ignorant than our worst educated agricultural labourers. They own and live on huge tracts of land, in most cases as large as a great English estate. Their method of living is many stages below that of our landless farm labourer. Their ignorance is colossal, their cupidity and cunning the envy of the Armenians, who openly confess that in a bargain the Russian peasant beats the Jew to a frazzle. The order of the Soviet Government to the peasants to take possession of the landowners' estates and property was the trump card which Lenin and Trotsky played to secure immunity in the provinces while they massacred and robbed the property owners in the towns. These men, who are the natural enemies of all political progress and social reform, and who should have exercised a steadying effect upon the empty idealism of the professional classes, were too busy robbing their neighbours to be able to exert any influence upon the major events of the revolution. While perfectly willing to use the revolution—whose principles they abhorred—for their own personal aggrandisement, this wealthy peasantry are now equally unwilling to render the slightest help in the restoration of order.

It was with profound interest that I read these documents, which entirely exploded the English legend of the landless Russian peasant pining for a few acres of land.

ARRIVAL OF THE BRITISH AT IRKUTSK.

Russian Labour

We arrived at Irkutsk and proceeded to investigate the situation. When we passed here four months before it was the centre of Siberian life; official indolence had, however, again reduced its status to that of a third- or fourth-rate town.

I was anxious to know how the new Rumanian Division under French auspices was progressing. Fourteen thousand rifles that could be ill afforded from the front had been left here some six weeks previous by one of our British supply trains. I found that the local Russian military authorities knew nothing, nor had they ever been consulted about it. They knew that not more than three thousand Rumanians lived in the district, and these had mostly embraced the opinions of the Bolsheviks. I made inquiries through the usual English channels, but they were equally uninformed. A visit to the Russian railway department elicited the fact that a French officer had signed the necessary orders for the trucks containing the rifles to remain at Irkutsk, that three thousand rifles had so far been unloaded, and that there was a French proposal to send the remainder to Tomsk, where it was hoped they might be got rid of amongst some Serbian bands with Bolshevik tendencies. This may or may not represent all the facts, but it indicates the unmistakable necessity that English help shall be given only by English hands.

Russian officers were beginning to recover their old characteristics, and nightly filled the entertainment halls and restaurants and led the gaieties of the town. Very little thought was given to the grim struggle their half-clad comrades were waging with the forces of anarchy along the Ural mountains.

British Consul Nash kindly entertained Colonel and Madame Frank and myself, and generally helped me in the organisation of this end of my campaign. He did not think much of my objective, but he helped all the same.

CHAPTER XVII

MY CAMPAIGN

I HELD my first meeting in the repairing shop at Irkutsk at 3 P.M., March 4. It was a big crowd of working men and women. The Russian women work on the railways in such employments as carriage and wagon cleaners, snow and ice shovellers, and even repairing gangs on different sections of the line have a sprinkling of the fair sex.

This audience listened to an explanation of the rise of the trade union movement in England with the greatest attention. The large majority accepted the proposition I tried to expound, that no question could be settled by the disputants merely killing each other off; but there were present about half a dozen members of the International World Workers, slouch-hatted, unshaven, and exactly true to type as seen at meetings in East London, Liverpool or Glasgow. These were not workmen employed on the railway; one kept a barber's shop, one was a teacher, one a Russian doctor, and one a Russian solicitor; but they were the officials of the only form of union that exists in Russian Siberia, a revolutionary circle composed of the very worst elements in the towns, bound together by one common purpose, the spolia- tion and assassination of every decent man, whether bourgeois or workman, who refuses to support a

183

policy of anarchy. These five or six determined ruffians formed a kind of Blood Brotherhood, and behind a veil of anonymity issued mandates to, and in the name of, the Russian workmen, which, backed up by a system of murderous terrorism, the workmen were powerless to resist. It was quite a usual thing to find each morning dead men of all classes in the streets who had been murdered during the night by members of these circles. There was no system of law or police; every vestige of justice was uprooted, and these crimes went unpunished. The irony of it was that these acts were avowedly done in the interest of progress and reform and in the sacred name of Labour!

The Irkutsk Circle asked questions which were not calculated to elicit a single fact connected with labour, either in Russia or England, but were just the usual clap-trap monkey business, such as:

" Why should we be satisfied with half, when we have the bourgeoisie down and can take all? "

" Why should we allow law to be re-established, which was always used by the few to rob the many? "

" Surely it is less unjust to allow the many to continue to rob the few? "

" In destroying the landlord and capitalist are not the Russian proletariat merely taking back its own property? "

" Is it not a fact that the more systematically and effectively we annihilate the bourgeois and landlord class, and all the institutions belonging to them, the easier it will be to erect the new order? "

These are all very subtle and difficult to answer

My Campaign

briefly at a meeting of Russian workmen, not one of whom can read or write. It was wonderful foresight which placed Madame Frank, the editress of the *Russian Army*, as correspondent for this labour mission. She fastened on to each question in turn and gave instance after instance of how the suggestions they contained had worked out in practice, to the total destruction of all that was good and honourable in Russia. Then with magnificent play on the words " the new order " in the last question, she drew a picture of this *new order* as exhibited in practice in that part of Russia under Bolshevik control. The influence of this little lady upon these simple Russian workmen was really remarkable. It was quite evident that the workmen would prefer the old régime to the new if Bolshevik tyranny is the only possible outcome of the new order.

Our next stop was Imokentievskaya, where the head of the works looked as though he would have preferred execution rather than take part in a workmen's meeting. The professionals had been left behind, and the audience was composed entirely of the railway workers. They presented many characteristics of the average English workmen and hungrily received information relating to the methods of the best organised English trade unions. They had no idea of the things we had done and the progress we had made in bettering the working conditions of labour generally. Their professional leaders had disposed of the British movement by describing our organisation as " bourgeois trade unions," and always referred to our trade union activities as though we were organised and internally managed by the capitalist. They were surprised to learn that we were the only exclusively working-class organisation in the world; that the officials must have worked at the trade whose society they managed; that we did not, like themselves, allow doctors, lawyers, and mere politicians to manage our affairs, but insisted upon having our trade unions in our own hands. One real old " Russky " engine-driver asked : " If the English workmen found it so advantageous to keep their organisations exclusively working-class, why did not the Germans do the same?" I answered, " When a movement starts wrong it is very difficult to put it right; that outsiders all over the world struggle for a place in the trade unions, and if once they get in they either break themselves or the union rather than get out, and those who can't get in hang on outside like limpets and refuse to be kicked off; that the Russian workmen in organising their trade unions must start right and keep them free of every element except the working class."

We stopped at Zema, the scene of a sharp encounter with armed strikers a few months previous. The meeting in the works was a great success. It was remarkable to find that though in my previous meeting with these workmen I took the attitude of a military dictator, they showed no resentment and had rigidly observed the agreement which had been entered into at the point of the bayonet. They were delighted to find that I, too, had performed my part of the contract in not forgetting their interests when opportunity presented itself.

My Campaign

Nesniodinsk was not on my list, but a special request having been presented for me to address the workmen there, we made the necessary arrangements and visited this place on Sunday, March 8. It was perhaps the largest meeting held up to that point. The official heads had caused a special platform to be erected in a huge engine-repairing shop, and themselves took the greatest interest in the whole proceeding. It was a very harassing business, but if as an outcome the seed of orderly progress was sown, the effort was entirely worth while.

Our carriage was fastened to the rear of a slow-moving train going west, and we did not arrive at Kansk till the evening of the 10th.

Kansk is the most easterly point of the area of revolt and a fairly large depot for the railway. Some interesting facts about the revolt were picked up from the railway officials. The revolt began suddenly on December 26, at the same time that it broke out in Omsk and Kolumsino, and at first was aimed at the possession of the railway. The military guard at Kansk consisted of one officer and fifty men. The officer posted his sentries at different points some distance away, and the soldiers who acted as his personal guard awoke to find their sleeping-place and arms in the possession of half a dozen armed men. The marauders shouted "Your officer is dead," and ordered the men to lie still while they removed the rifles. This done, they proceeded to the quarters of the officer, who, finding his men already disarmed, bolted without firing a shot. The total strength of the Bolsheviks was fifteen men, and these fifteen held

With the "Die-Hards" in Siberia

the station and a town of over five thousand inhabitants up to ransom for twenty-six hours! At the end of that time a squadron of Cossacks approached, and the Bolsheviks left, taking with them about 80,000 roubles belonging to the railway and post office. During their short stay they committed all sorts of barbarities. They murdered the railway schoolmistress and tortured her husband by stripping him and pouring cold water over his naked body, finally driving him out into the snow, where he quickly froze to death. The charge against their two victims in this case was that they, by their calling, were teaching the youth of Russia to become young *bourgeoisie*, instead of leaving all men and women equal as nature intended.

This garden of autocracy grows some strange plants. These banditti, known in England as Bolsheviks, are entrenched not more than 60 versts distant, protected from Koltchak's vengeance by the deep snows of the Siberian winter, which make it impossible to operate away from the railway.

We held a splendid meeting of the workmen in the enormous workshop, remarkable for the quiet enthusiasm and the evident hope of better times. It was quite clear to me that the Russian workmen were tired of the Revolution. They were promised an Eldorado and realised Hell instead. They merely wanted to be shown a way out of the social nightmare. They passed a vote of thanks to me and the English workmen for whom I spoke.

We started for Krasnoyarsk on the 12th, and before long found it necessary to get the machine

My Campaign

guns and hospital equipment ready for instant use. After standing to arms all night we arrived, at midday on the 13th, at Klukvinah, the Russian Headquarters, and discovered that the Government forces had driven the enemy back from the railway, and that the remainder of our journey to Krasnoyarsk would be practically safe. We arrived about 9.15 P.M. on Wednesday, the 13th.

Colonel Frank, Madame Frank, myself and the Czech interpreter, Vladimir, were passing through the station on our return from the town about 12.30 midnight, when a rather exciting incident occurred. The station commandant approached Colonel Frank and appealed to him for help to send home a party of Serbian soldiers who had procured drink without payment at the point of their swords and revolvers, and had stripped a young woman passenger and exposed her for their orgies. Other bestial things were alleged against them, but no one had so far dared to interfere to restore order. After a moment's consideration Colonel Frank decided to go into the buffet and ask them to go quietly home, and if they refused, to secure force to arrest and remove them. I naturally followed.

It was a big stone-floored room with the door at one end and a long bar at the other. The alleged Serbian soldiers were seated in a cluster on the right in front of the bar at the far end of the room. Colonel Frank advanced to them and said, " Brothers, you have had enough to drink, you are keeping all the attendants from their proper rest ; it is time for you to go home." It was like an electric shock. About

189

a dozen of the ruffians sprang to their feet hurling every possible Slavonic epithet at this brave Russian officer who was merely performing a public duty. One dark-visaged Serb cavalryman drew his sword and tried a lunge at the colonel across the table, and while the colonel watched this infuriated aborigine a Serbian officer close behind Frank tore the epaulette from the colonel's uniform and trampled it underfoot, shouting, "Death to this officer of the old régime!"

I picked up the epaulette just as the other Serb, sword in one hand and revolver in the other, edged round the tables to the centre of the room for his attack upon my liaison officer. I did not think of drawing my own weapon, and so far it was man to man. Colonel Frank kept his eye fixed upon his antagonist, and now advanced towards him, ordering him to put down his arms and leave the room. But the Serb was out for blood and made a slash at the *polkovnika's* head, the full force of which he evaded by ducking, though the sword severed the chin strap and button of his cap and carved its way through the thick band before it glanced up off the skull, helped by his right hand, which had been raised to turn the blow. At the same instant Colonel Frank fired point blank at the man's face; the bullet entered the open mouth and came out of the cheek, which merely infuriated the man more. Up to this moment the man had only used his sword, but now he began to raise his revolver. Before he could raise it hip high, however, the colonel shot him through the heart. Though the revolver dropped from his helpless hand, he crouched for one instant and sprang, clutching at the colonel's

My Campaign

face, while four or five of his fellow Serbs attacked the colonel from behind. The foremost of these ruffians, a Serbian officer, fired at the back of the colonel's head and missed, but his second shot struck Colonel Frank on the left temple at the moment his real assailant had made his death spring, and down they both went, apparently dead, the Serbian on top. The other Serbs sprang forward to finish the Russian officer with the usual ugly dagger which Serbian robbers always carry. The body of the dead Serb, however, formed a complete shield, and this, coupled with the fact that we all thought the colonel dead, saved him from mutilation.

I was not quite an idle spectator, but the fact that at the critical moment I discovered I had no weapon except for my cane reduced me to helplessness so far as dealing with this gang of murderers was concerned. Directly the fight began every Russian, including the armed militiaman who was supposed to keep order at the station, bolted from the room, leaving the women and children to look after themselves. Madame Frank went to the assistance of her husband and covered him as only a woman can, and as she grasped her husband's revolver the Serbs slunk back a pace, while I lifted his head and signed to the Serb officer who had fired at the colonel from behind to lift the dead Serb off the colonel's body. This he did and then proposed to the band surrounding us that they should kill us all three. Their knives glistened and a small automatic revolver was making a bee line for me, when a voice like the growl of a bear came from the direction of the door.

With the "Die-Hards" in Siberia

The whole band instantly put up their weapons. I had stood up to receive my fate, and over the heads of our would-be murderers I saw a tall dark-bearded stage villain in a long black overcoat which reached to the floor, stalk across to the group. He looked at the body of the dead Serb and then at the prostrate Russian officer who at that instant began to show signs of returning consciousness. "Ah! Oh! Russky polkovnik," he roared, drawing his revolver. "Our dead brother demands blood."

I could not stand and see a wounded friend murdered before my eyes, not even in this land of blood. I stepped over both bodies and placed myself between this monster and his victim. I raised both hands and pushed him back, saying, "I am Anglisky polkovnik, and will not allow you to murder the wounded Russian officer." He answered that he was "Serbian polkovnik," and I said "Come into the other room," and by strategy got him away. His friends, however, told him something which sent him back quickly to finish his job, but as he re-entered the buffet he encountered about a dozen British and Czech soldiers with fixed bayonets, and it was not so difficult now to convince him that it was not quite good form to murder a wounded man.

We carried the Russian colonel to the British hospital, and as the leader of the Serbs had declared a blood feud, extra guards were placed on my wagon and the hospital. These ruffians were armed from our supplies under the direction of French officers. Directly the Russian military authorities began their investigations to bring this band to justice they,

My Campaign

through the Czech commander, received orders from General Ganin, the French Allied commander, to move to Novo Nikoliosk out of Russian jurisdiction.

It is not very clear at present why the French gave their protection to these and similar disturbing elements in Siberia. Perhaps the reason will show itself later.

Krasnoyarsk is a huge railway depot with building and repairing shops employing about 3,000 workmen. To get at both shifts it was necessary to hold two meetings, one for the inside and the other for the outside staff. The first was a very silent, interested crowd, who listened to my address as though they understood its meaning and purport. The gallant "Russky" *polkovnika* with bandaged head and hand translated the first part, Madame Frank the second. The impression created by this brave woman, who had herself commanded a company in the trenches before Kerensky destroyed the army, was very great. There was no mistaking the effect of her words as these oil-stained workmen raised their *papahas* to the message from the English trade unionists which she delivered.

This town was the centre of international intrigue. There was an Italian battalion about 1,500 strong, the Czech 12th Regiment of about 200, and the British Middlesex Regiment, 220. To maintain their prestige the French were arming the Lett revolters as fast as the Russian General Affinasiaff could defeat and disarm them. The Italian soldiers were in very bad favour with the inhabitants and the local Russian civil and military authorities. Robberies and assaults were of almost daily occurrence, and at last the authorities made definite official complaints to the Allied Headquarters and asked that the Italian soldiers should either be kept under proper discipline or removed from the country. The main complaint, however, of the Russian officials was based on the open hostility of the Allied officers led by the senior of them to everything Russian.

It is such an easy matter to make friends with the Russian people that this attitude of her alleged helpers was very saddening. When I landed at "Vlady" my orders were to remember that we English had come as friends to help Russia on to her feet, and I always tried to keep that in mind. I often wondered what instructions could have been given to my Allied colleagues.

The next call was at Bogotol, where, under instructions from Consul Peacock, I inquired into the imprisonment of an Australian subject named Savinoff. The authorities produced the *dossier* of his case, which when translated proved him to be a Bolshevik leader and second in command of an armed band that had attempted to murder the local authorities. His trial took place shortly after, with that of Titoff, his chief, who was one of the Central Committee of the Baltic Fleet who ordered the murder of hundreds of the naval officers of the old régime.

The meeting maintained the usual standard of interest, and the chief of the works, whose face bore traces of the tortures inflicted upon him under Bolshevik rule, was delighted with the new hope we had brought to himself and his workmen.

My Campaign

Our next meeting was at Taiga, and it was quite a great event. A special platform had been erected in the big workshop, around which swarmed nearly two thousand workmen. The people looked upon the meeting as the new birth of Russian life. No meeting had been held for two years, except the underground gatherings of conspirators. I appealed to the men to discard disorder and take a hand in the orderly reconstruction of the new Russian State, in which they were now guaranteed a place. Madame Frank's translation made a profound impression upon these toil-worn men and women. It was clear that the people were tired of the horrors of revolution and yearned for peace and quiet.

I here interviewed General Knox, who was on his way to Omsk on important matters which had been brought to my notice.

We arrived at Novo Nikoliosk on the morning of the 23rd, and proceeded to make arrangements for the meeting to be held on the same day. I visited the various commands, as usual, and held long consultations with General Zochinko, from whom I gathered much information as to the situation in this important district. It was interesting to hear some news of our old friend, the *Voidavoda* of the Serbian band. He and his gang had arrived from his excursion to Krasnoyarsk on the day that a banquet was held by the newly-formed Polish regiment. As chief of his band he was invited, and delivered an oration of a particularly patriotic character which had won all Polish hearts. He was in a great hurry to get away next morning, fearing that we were following behind. He said nothing about our encounter, and the Russian officials became suspicious of his anxiety to get away. They brought a squad of soldiers to examine his trucks, and found an enormous amount of loot from Krasnoyarsk, as well as contraband goods upon which he had to pay duty to the amount of 130,000 roubles. Having squeezed this toll out of the "bounder," they gave him a free way to Ekaterinburg, where things are very scarce, and where he would be able to sell out at a good figure.

General Zochinko told us some funny stories about the French Staff's attempt to form a powerful counter force to Bolshevism from the German and Austrian war prisoners. In Novo Nikoliosk the Allied Commander, General Ganin, had released some hundreds of Austrian and German Poles from the prison camps and formed them into regiments. In his haste to get these units complete he forgot to inquire into the antecedents of the officers chosen to command them. So careless, in fact, were the French that the Russian authorities awoke one morning to find one of their most dangerous prisoners, a well-known German officer spy, von Budburg, in full command of this alleged Allied force. Von Budburg had, like a true patriot, taken care to choose his subordinates from men of the same type as himself.

Later on the French Staff became aware of the nature of their handiwork and sought help and advice from the Russian military authorities about disarming their new German Legion. A sudden descent on their quarters by another Polish unit, with some new Russian units standing by to render help if neces-

My Campaign

sary, ended in these French protégés being disarmed and got back safely to their prison camp.

Allied help to Russia is like a jig-saw puzzle, a mystery even to the man who devised it. A straight-forward recognition of the Omsk Government would have been an honest hand for honest work, but where would Allied diplomacy have come in? Diplomacy is only necessary when there are ulterior objects than mere plain, unambiguous assistance to a helpless friend. What are these hidden objects? The Allies had better be cautious how they proceed in the diagnosis and dismemberment of this great people or they may find themselves on the operating table with this giant holding the knife. In spite of the Biblical legend I prefer England to be a pal with Goliath!

We arrived at Barabinsk on the morning of March 26, and after arrangements for the meeting were completed, took a walk round the market. A Russian market is a thing of joy and colour. There are no buildings : just a huge space in the centre of the town where thousands of shaggy, ice-covered horses stand each with an ice-covered sledge. The peasants, men and women, in huge fur coats which reach to the snow-covered ground, harmonise perfectly with the cattle they control. Their fur coats form a study in colour—patchwork coats from calfskins which combine every shade from white to rusty red ; goatskins, from long straight black to white ; curly bearskins from black to brown and brown to po.. white ; wealthy peasant women, with beautif.l red fox furs hiding neck and face, their eyes glistening through the apertures which served t... ...urpose

N   197

for the first and original tenant. The sledges contain everything—wheat, oats, potatoes, onions, rough leaf tobacco, jars of cream, frozen blocks of milk, scores of different types of frozen fresh-water fish from sturgeon to bream, frozen meats of every conceivable description, furs—in fact, the finest collection of human necessities to be found in any one place in the world. Prices were very high for home produce and simply absurd for foreign or distant productions. Colonel Frank was in need of a small safety pin (six a penny at home), and found that the price was seven roubles—14s. 3½d. old money, and 3s. 6d. at the rate at which the British Army are paid. Everything else was in proportion.

A very fine meeting was held in the works, and much good done in securing the confidence of the workmen in the efforts of the Supreme Governor, Admiral Koltchak, to create order out of chaos.

We arrived at Omsk on the morning of the 28th, and on the 29th I gave a lengthy report to Admiral Koltchak, who expressed his hearty thanks and impressed upon me the necessity of continuing my journey to the Urals. He had received from the official heads of departments reports stating that the effect of my mission had been to improve the general attitude of the workmen all round. And he was most anxious that this effort to enlist the workmen's interest in an ordered State should be pushed forward with vigour.

A further discussion upon general affairs, especially the policy of the French command in Siberia, took us through tea. I have absolute confidence in the character of the admiral, but the pigmies by whom he is surrounded are so many drags on the wheels of State. There is not one that I would trust to manage a whelk-stall. They have no idea of the duty of a statesman. Little pettifogging personal equations and jobs occupy the whole of their time, except when they are engaged upon the congenial task of trying to thwart the Supreme Governor. The patriotism of the front officers and soldiers, and the medieval chivalry of the Cossack are the only things left upon which to rebuild Russia. This naturally limits the architectural features of the new edifice, but the pioneer is always limited to the material at hand.

CHAPTER XVIII

It is quite interesting to watch the oscillation of the Omsk mind from one orientation to another. At the time I left for the East the stream of favour flowed strongly in the English direction. General Knox started on a tour of Siberia in connection with the formation of the new Koltchak army; Sir Charles Eliot went to Hong-Kong; General Bowes was left to deputise for General Knox, and Colonel Robertson for Sir Charles Eliot. In three short weeks every sign of British influence had disappeared. The English were nowhere; the favour was shared equally by France and Japan.

The Japanese had either learned how to behave themselves towards the Russians or they had received instructions from home. During the first three months I was in Siberia their arrogance was simply sublime, but after the armistice with Germany—upon whose power to defeat the Allies they banked their all—they were a changed people, so far as outward appearance and conduct were concerned. They talked about their alliance with England, their friendship with Russia, their love of France. When the Japanese try, they can make themselves very agreeable; indeed, so charming that it is impossible to resist their advances. That was their attitude then

Omsk Re-visited

to all except the Chinese, whom they hold in the greatest contempt, and to the Americans, whom they fear. With a clear field their new policy made great headway.

The French methods are quite different. Theirs is a drawing-room attack, and at this sort of thing the ordinary Britisher cuts but a sorry figure. Hence the field was also pretty clear for them, and they made full use of their opportunities. With a judicious word over a cup of tea an editor who refuses a bribe finds his or her talents a glut on the market. A joke around a *samovar* reduces the rank of a particularly Russophile general. The glorious time they are having reaches its climax when you hear the polite condolences to the victims uttered in exquisite French.

But Colonel Robertson had gone to " Vlady," and his place had been taken by a typical Britisher in the person of Consul Hodgson, who took a correct measure of the situation, and in less than forty-eight hours herded the whole caboose back into their own compounds. It is surprising that the influence of one virile, definite personality can be so great, and it proves how necessary it is that in this seemingly endless turmoil only the best men should be burdened with the responsibility of our representation. I started on my mission to the Urals with absolute confidence that, in the absence of General Knox, our interests in Omsk would not suffer so long as they were in the hands of our senior consul.

After infinite trouble with Russian official elements, I started on my western journey on

With the "Die-Hards" in Siberia

April 5. The mission consisted of Colonel Frank (liaison officer), Madame Frank (translator), Regt-Sergt.-Major Gordon, in charge of an escort of twenty-two N.C.O.s and men, with one machine gun. We were now entering the district behind the Ural front. These towns had not long been cleared of the Bolsheviks, so that it was interesting to discover how far their ideas had gained possession of the minds of the people. The new Russian armies were rapidly pushing forward. Their progress had been made more general and persistent since the end of November, 1918, the date on which the Czechs finally refused to take part in the great Perm offensive. When they read in the English papers of January, 1919, how the Czech, Italian, French, and Allied forces had inflicted defeat upon the Bolsheviks at Perm, it caused a grim smile to pass over the faces of the Russian officers who did the job. Not a single Czech, Italian, French, or Allied soldier fired a shot after Admiral Koltchak assumed supreme command. There is one notable exception. The armoured trains from H.M.S. *Suffolk*, under the command of Captain Wolfe Murray, continued to fight along the Ufa front well into January, 1919. Only the intense cold and the necessity of recoupment and re-equipment caused them to retire to Omsk. The British Navy fighting on the Urals was the only reminder the Russian soldier had that the Allies of his country had not entirely deserted her.

We arrived at Tumen on April 7, and held a fine meeting of the workmen, who seemed quite pleased to hear that the Bolsheviks were not likely

Omsk Re-visited

to return. These workmen looked upon the Bolshevik rule as on some horrible nightmare. They cared for little else so long as you could assure them on this point. So ghastly was the dream from which they had awakened compared with the flowery promises held out to them that I readily believe " Ivan the Terrible " would have been received at that moment as a saviour. This was a dangerous feeling which I tried my best to combat, for the excesses of the Bolshevik régime have prepared the way—and were deliberately intended so to do—for a return to absolutism.

We arrived at Ekaterinburg at the same time as General Knox arrived from Chilliyabinsk. His first words were congratulations on my C.B., news of which had just arrived. I visited Consul Preston, and read the evidence he and his French colleague had collected relative to Bolshevik outrages on the workmen of the district. It was too sad to think about. This was the place where the Tsar and his family were imprisoned and murdered. Of them it could be fairly alleged that they were responsible for the crimes of the old régime; but what crimes have the poor workmen and peasants committed that the most fiendish cruelty should be reserved for them? I give it up ! Perhaps there is some reason or justification; all I can say is I have not heard it, neither can I imagine what it can be.

I held a meeting of railway workmen and officials, and was surprised at the attention and earnestness of the audience. They hungrily devoured every scrap of information as to our English trade union organisation and work, and requested that a further meeting should be held next day in a great carriage works in the centre of the town. This proved to be one of the most remarkable gatherings I have ever attended. A fine platform had been erected at one end of the main workshop. A sea of faces under huge multi-coloured *papahas* spread over the floor, while every carriage was covered with human ants; even the beams of the building carried its human freight. Clearly it seemed to me that the resurrection of Russia had begun; the destruction of Russia began from the head, its re-birth is from the ground.

CHAPTER XIX

IN EUROPEAN RUSSIA

NEVANISK is situated just over the European boundary of the Urals. Before the Bolshevik came it was a great iron centre, one firm alone employing three thousand workmen. When I arrived there the various works were practically derelict and its vast collection of machinery idle. The streets were deserted, and it was estimated that half of its inhabitants had been destroyed. It was, and now it is not. The few remaining inhabitants were valiantly pulling themselves together, and if order and some sort of law could be established, they were confident that they could rebuild their life again. We talked to them and encouraged them to continue their struggle against the blight that had defiled their homes and their country. Their hopes seemed to revive from our assurance of English working-class sympathy. I am pleased they did not know that we had some people mad enough to wish to inflict similar wounds upon our own country.

A pound of sugar cost thirty-five roubles, a pair of 3s. 11d. goloshes two hundred and fifty roubles, one pound of bread seven roubles. These were the things we wished to buy, and so made the discovery of their price; we bought bread only, as the thing we could not do without. Typhus was raging in almost every house. General Knox was inoculated, but I decided to run the risk. Doctors had largely disappeared, owing to the hatred of everybody with a bourgeois education.

I wonder what sort of jokes or fun G.B.S. could make out of it. There *is* fun in it somewhere. The contrast between the original idea of the revolution and the outcome of those ideas are so grotesque in their realisation that it looks as though some hidden power were indulging in a Mephistophelian laugh at the expense of mankind.

We next arrived at Taighill, where the same effects had been produced, though on a smaller scale. It was Palm Sunday, and the great bell of the cathedral was booming through the surrounding pine forest calling the faithful to prayer. In the square of the town near by a statue of Alexander II lay in the mud, having been thrown down by the revolutionaries. Quite near a white figure of a woman, intended to represent the Enthronement of Liberty, had been hurled from its recently constructed base, and formed the roadside seat of five or six of the raggedest starvelings to be found in the world. An inscription on Alexander's statue states that it was raised to commemorate his emancipation of the peasants from serfdom. The Bolsheviks had not time to write *their* inscription; but it did not matter —the empty houses and deserted streets were quite enough. By means of much elbow labour they had smoothed out the inscription on the statue of the Tsar Liberator and for the time made all things equal again.

In European Russia

The meeting at Taighill was a repetition of the others, and we passed on to Kushva. This place had been badly mauled. The Bolshevik Commissar was evidently an anarchist pure and simple. All the hatred of class and creed which had generated under the Romanoffs found expression in this man's deeds. The amount of venom which he put into his administration and work was worthy of his cause. The effect of his policy, however, produced results exactly opposite to those he hoped for. The first evidence of his zeal lay upon the snow in front of the railway office. A huge steel safe with the door wrenched off and the contents missing indicated the strength of his principles. The official who had lost the key was thrown into the well near by to stimulate the memory of other safe-owners; but this official was not alone in his glory, for several railway workmen who refused to help rob this identical safe found a watery grave with their superior. Altogether over seventy people met their death in this well, workmen, *bourgeoisie* —all in one holocaust. But the majority were of no class; their only offence seemed to be that they had called themselves Social Revolutionaries. They have been the subject of the most bitter hatred by the Bolshevik leaders. The Bolshevik contention is that for men or women to call themselves Socialists, and then to hesitate to take a hand in the complete extermination of the bourgeois ruling classes, now there is a chance of doing so in Russia, is to act the part of poltroon and traitor to the cause. The " treachery " is all the greater if the objector is a workman or a workwoman.

With the " Die-Hards " in Siberia

The Bolsheviks are quite honest about their purpose—the transfer of power and property by murder and robbery from the *bourgeoisie* to the proletariat. If a member of the proletariat is so mad that he refuses or hesitates to act his part in this scheme, then those who have been called by the force of events to assume a dictatorship on his behalf are entitled to destroy him as an unconscious enemy to himself and his class. In the same way no mercy can be shown to the Social Revolutionaries who, while professing allegiance to definite proletarian domination, shrink from definite action now that the time for action has arrived.

The Bolshevik Commissar of Kushva, acting on this principle, succeeded in a short time in raising a formidable opposition amongst the workmen in the surrounding districts. When the local schoolmistress, a girl of seventeen, found a temporary grave in this sort of Black Hole of Calcutta the wells of Kushva and Taighill became a dreadful portent to the simple Russian *mujik*.

The opposition began at the big Watkin Works, where over six thousand men were employed. Though possessing no military organisation, the workmen decided to resist by force the entrance of the Bolshevik Terror into their midst. With the help of several young engineers they managed to regiment themselves into some kind of military order. They selected with great skill the strategic positions for fortifications, and held the whole district against the repeated attacks of the enemy. Once the Bolshevik line of the Urals west of Ekaterinburg

In European Russia

struck from north to south, from Kunghure to the Caspian, as the crow flies, for three thousand versts, except for one great loop enclosing the Watkin Works. But in November, 1918, the Bolshevik line swept forward, submerging these valiant workmen warriors. Admiral Koltchak's Chief of Staff naturally concluded that the workmen had given up the struggle and had made terms ,with their hated enemy.

This surge forward of the Bolsheviks had been greatly assisted by the unfortunate defection of the Czech forces, who had left the front at the suggestion of their local National Council. General Gaida had thrown up his Czech commission, and had been given command of the right wing of the new Russian army. The admiral proceeded at once to put his new army to the test by an attempt to recover the lost ground and, if possible, save the remnants of the Watkin workmen. Everybody now knows how, in a temperature of over " 60 below," these recently mobilised Siberian recruits re-established the fighting fame of the Russian soldier by sweeping the Terrorist forces from their positions and entirely destroying them at Perm. Imagine General Galitzin's surprise when the advance began to find these Watkin workmen still holding their district and rendering valuable help to their relieving comrades! The Kushva Soviet Commissar had built better than he knew.

This district is remarkable for the valuable and extensive deposits of iron and sulphur, which seem inexhaustible. One huge hill has a store of about 800,000,000,000 tons, almost untapped except

With the " Die-Hards " in Siberia

for uncovering work necessary to estimate its capacity.

The Revolution in Russia may alter a few things, but it can scarcely effect much change in the character of its people. This iron mountain is an illustration of the mixture of mediævalism and modernism to be found in Russia's industrial development. The summit of the mountain is capped with an Orthodox Greek church, and desperate efforts have been made to secure its removal to a less exalted and less valuable site. I was informed that the mere suggestion proved almost fatal to its originators, and by so narrow a margin did they escape that the proposal is not likely to be repeated. I made the suggestion quite innocently, and produced such a storm that only my foreign ignorance provided me with a satisfactory excuse. I was asked : " Would you take God from His place over this work? " One other thing I noticed everywhere. There was not one important workshop from Irkutsk to Perm without its altar, candles and all complete, and scarcely a business or Government office without its ikon facing you the moment you entered.

I attended the Orthodox Easter celebration at Perm. The whole edifice was crowded with people of every walk in life. I was not merely an interested spectator, but one who believes that where man worships he appeals to the same God no matter by what name He is called.

I watched this crowd, each holding a long lighted taper, stand for hours making the sign of the Cross, while the gorgeously-robed priest chanted the service

and made sundry waves with his hands and gave
certain swings with the incense-burner. The
responses were made by a group of men with
beautiful, well-trained voices, but the people looked
spiritually starved. Not one took the slightest part
in the service beyond an occasional whispered
murmur, nor are they expected to. They stood outside the pale; there was no place for them. I must
say that I contrasted this isolation of the congrega-
tion with the joint act of worship as performed in
our churches, both Free and Anglican. I looked at
these " Christian " men and women and thought of
the butchery of Petrograd and Moscow, the wells
of Kushva and Taighill, and the ruthless disregard
of human life by both sides in this brutal internecine
strife. I wondered whether I had stumbled upon
at least one of the causes. At any rate, I did not
forget we also had the heroes of the Watkin Works.

Nadegenska is the extreme north-west point of
the Ural system of railways, and is famous because
of its great privately-owned steelworks. These works
were originated by a poor peasant woman, who
developed the whole district until it has become the
most northerly Asiatic industrial centre in the
Russian Empire. The contrast in treatment at these
privately-owned works compared with those owned
by the Government is significant. The Soviet Commissar knew nothing about the business himself, and
appointed Works Commissars, still more ignorant of
their duties, to control the establishment. The result
was that production fell to such a point that the
experts refused to work under such incompetents and

gradually escaped to other outlandish districts. The
manager stuck to his post during the battle of Perm,
and by a judicious distribution among the Bolshevik
Commissars of the surplus roubles of the Tsar
remaining in his possession got them out of the works
without damage. This was an unheard-of situation,
for nowhere else have the Soviet Commissars left
anything they could destroy.

It ,was interesting to notice that nearly the whole
of the machinery in these works was either of German
or American make, the latter always predominating ;
there was some English and some Belgian, about an
equal amount of each. I heard a curious statement
at Kushva to the effect that the German firms were
always prepared to build and fit out a big works, and
run it for one year, without asking for a penny. Of
course they always first carefully examined the possibilities of the locality, but the managers assured me
that it was rare for German machinery to be equal,
either for use or wear and tear, to the English, nor
was it as cheap ; but they could always get long
credit from German firms, and that was most
important in developing new enterprises.

We set off for Perm, with a stop on our way
at the Vackneah Turansky Works. These works
employed from four to five thousand men, doing
everything from smelting to the making of engines,
carriages, shells, guns, etc., and were the best
equipped workshops I saw in the Urals. The only
complaint was lack of orders. The old régime did
everything--nearly all this great mineral district was
developed under the personal care of the Tsars. The

In European Russia

Bolsheviks have destroyed the State control of these establishments, and already the *bourgeoisie* are casting hungry eyes upon this great industry and the Omsk Ministers are rubbing hands over the loot they hope to collect during this transfer. How vain the hopes of those who looked to the Revolution to develop public control of all natural resources! Already the State lands are parcelled out amongst the wealthy peasants, who as a result of this robbery will establish a great landed aristocracy, and, if I do not misread the signs, a similar fate is about to overtake the great State industries with the creation of an aristocracy of wealth.

At Turansky we picked up Sergeant Coleman, of the Durham Light Infantry, the only Englishman who weathered the journey from Archangel with a party of Russians who had started from the north to try and get into direct touch with the Russian Army. They had made a circuitous route and avoided the districts held by the Bolshevik forces, and therefore had nothing of interest to report to us. The whole party, under a Russian officer in English uniform, were attached to my train and taken to Perm, where instructions awaited them to proceed at once to Omsk.

While examining the damage done during the street fighting at Perm we encountered a mob of the Red Guard who had marched over their own lines at Glashoff and surrendered to General Gaida. They were drawn up four deep in the market-place for a roll call. I studied their faces and general appearance, and came to the conclusion that if the progress

o   213

of the world depended upon such as these the world was in a very bad way. They were Kirghis, Mongols, Tartars, Chinese, mixed with a fair sprinkling of European-Russian peasants, workmen and others mostly of the lowest type, but with just enough of the " old soldier " element to make them formidable. A strange idea struck me that I would like to speak to these men. The proposition, made almost in jest, was taken up seriously by my liaison officer, Colonel Frank, who interviewed the commandant of the station, Colonel Nikolioff, upon the subject. He at first took up a hostile attitude, but when he gathered the substance of my proposed address he consented, and arranged the meeting at the camp for 6 P.M. the following evening, April 22. Of all the meetings it has been my privilege to hold, this was the most unique. The Bolshevik soldiers stood to attention and listened to me with great interest. One or two were sailors, and some others could understand a little English, as could be seen by the way they conveyed in whispers the points of the speech to their neighbours. Madame Frank translated, and in beautiful Russian drove home each point. Hers was a magnificent performance. As she repeated my word-picture of their untilled fields, destroyed homes, outraged women, and murdered children, not the ravages of an alien enemy, but the work of their own hands, Russian against Russian, tears trickled down their war-scarred faces. Clearly these men felt they had been deceived, and would willingly endeavour to rectify the injuries of the past. Some volunteered their services at once to help their

In European Russia

Mother Country to recover from the ravages they had made and administer justice upon those who had led them into madness, but Colonel Nikolioff asked them to remember that their crimes had been very great, and nothing but time could heal the wounds and soften the bitterness their conduct had created. Some asked that it should be remembered that they were not Bolshevik in principle, but had been forced to become soldiers in the Red Army, from which they could not desert until their villages were captured by the Koltchak army, as their whole families, held as hostages for their good conduct, would have been massacred. This they asserted had been done in numberless cases where the families were in Bolshevik hands.

The value of the rouble in Perm at that time was about one penny. My officers and men were paid at the rate of 40 roubles to the £1. The prisoners' camp was about three and a half versts distant, and the duration of the meeting was one hour and five minutes; the droshky hire for the journey was 100 roubles per droshky. Everything was in proportion. For instance, common cigarettes were 1 rouble each. If I had smoked twenty a day or used them between myself and my numerous official visitors, half my colonel's pay would have gone. There must surely have been something wrong in fixing the rate of exchange at Harbin or " Vlady," 5,000 versts away, and leaving officers at the front in a stage of poverty not one whit better than the people whose all had been destroyed by the Revolution. I have no remedy to

With the " Die-Hards " in Siberia

offer, but it is not very satisfactory to receive your
rouble at 6d. and spend it at 1d. What is more!
If I had been paid in £1 notes or sovereigns, I could
have got something approaching 200 roubles for each
at the Perm rate! Wages had increased under
Bolshevik rule, but prices were such that one of the
petitions we had to forward to the Government at
Omsk on behalf of the workmen was that the wages
and prices should be the same as under the old
régime.

On April 24 the ice on the Khama started to
move about 5 A.M. It was a very imposing sight.
It moved first as one solid block, carrying boats,
stacks of timber, sledge roads—everything—with it.
The point near the bridge held for some time, until
the weight behind forced some part down and
crunched its way through in one irresistible push;
the other part rose over the resistance and rolled like
an avalanche over and over, smashing itself into huge
blocks which were forced into a rampart fifty feet
high, when the enormous weight broke the ice platform on which it was piled, and the whole moved
majestically off towards the Volga. Then one ex-
perienced the peculiar illusion of gliding along the
river; it was necessary to plant one's feet far apart
to prevent a fall. The Khama near Perm is over
a mile wide, and this method of Nature to herald
spring to these snow- and ice-bound regions lacks
nothing so far as grandeur is concerned. During
the next few days millions of tons of derelict timber
passed on its way to the Caspian. The careless
Russian never thinks of hauling his spare stock off

the ice until the ice actually begins to move. He tells you that the proper time for the ice to move is between May 1 and 5; that if it moves a week earlier it means good crops, which would balance the loss of the timber, so that he has no cause to complain.

It is no part of my business to deal with atrocities such as have disgraced the proletarian dictatorship of Moscow. Where I could not avoid them in my narrative of events, I have done so without reference to the revolting details which everybody so hungrily devours. History shows that it is not possible to avoid these excesses whenever the safeguards of civil order are swept away by the passions of the mob. Our own revolutionaries should remember this before and not after the event. They should be considered not as a risk but as a certainty when once the foundations of order are uprooted. At Perm the breaking of the ice revealed some of the truth, and it formed quite sufficient evidence of the callous behaviour of the Bolshevik administrators.

Below a steep bank a few yards from the Terrorist headquarters a small shed was erected on the ice. It was called a wash-house, and during the day washing was done there. At night the place, apparently, was, like the streets, deserted, but as a square hole was cut through the ice, it was an ideal place for the disposal of bodies, dead or alive. The people knew that after an inspection of the better-class homes by officers of the Soviet if there was evidence of valuable loot; the whole family would quietly disappear, and the valuables were distributed by sale, or otherwise, amongst the Soviet authorities.

With the " Die-Hards " in Siberia

If a workman protested against this violence, he disappeared, too, in the same secret fashion.

The poor women who used the shed during the day for its legitimate purpose told from time to time grim stories of blood and evidence of death struggles on the frozen floor as they began the morning's work. Several thousand people were missing by the time the Koltchak forces captured the town.

The ice in the shelter of the bank began to thaw before the more exposed part of the river, which enabled the people whose friends and neighbours were missing to put a rude and ineffective screen below the shed in the hope of recovering the bodies of some of their friends. I knew about the shed but not about the screen, until I was informed by Regt. Sergeant-Major Gordon that he had seen several hundred bodies taken from the river. The following morning I walked into the crowd of anxious people who were watching the work. The official in charge told me quite simply that they had not had a very good morning, for three hours' work had only produced some forty bodies. I looked at these relics of the new order; they were of both sexes and belonged to every condition of life, from the gruff, horny-handed worker to the delicately-nurtured young girl. A miscellaneous assortment of the goods, among other things, revolutions are bound to deliver.

We held a big meeting in the great railway works which created quite a sensation. The fact that the English were at Perm spread back to Omsk, and four days later Japanese and French Missions put in an appearance. If the French came to maintain their

In European Russia

prestige it was a pity that they did not choose a better agent for their purpose. I had been invited to lunch with a very worthy representative of the town, Mr. Pastrokoff, and his wife. I arrived to find the good lady in great agitation. A French officer had called and informed the household that a French Mission had just arrived composed of three officers; they would require the three best rooms in the house, the use of the servants and kitchen; that no furniture must be removed from the three rooms he saw under pain of punishment, etc. The lady protested and told the French officer that even the Bolsheviks had not demanded part of her very small house when made acquainted with the requirements of her family, but the officer had replied that any inconvenience was outweighed by the great honour conferred upon her house by the presence of officers of the French Army. It would not be polite to the glorious French Army to repeat Madame Pastrokoff's reply. It only shows how stupid it is to send to foreign countries any but the best men to represent a great and gallant nation. I naturally reminded Madame that she was a Russian, living in her own country, under her own Government, and she must report the case to the Russian authorities, who would doubtless provide accommodation for the French Mission if necessary.

The Pastrokoffs, coupled with the vivacious Madame Barbara Pastokova and her husband, were among the most homely and interesting people it was my pleasure to meet in the Urals. If you have never been in Russia you know nothing of hospitality; you only squirm around the fringe of the subject.

With the " Die-Hards " in Siberia

The hospitality of our friends at Perm was truly Russian, and I was sorry when we had to leave. M. Pastrokoff told me of the following incident of the early relief of Perm from the Terrorist.

General Pepolieff's army was stretched along the railway from Perm towards Vatka, the junction of the Archangel Railway. The temperature was over " 60 below," the men were without clothes, thousands had died from exposure, and other thousands were in a ghastly condition from frost-bite. There was little or no hospital accommodation, and the Omsk Ministers were deaf to all appeals for help, they being more concerned as to how they could shake off the Supreme Governor's control than how best to perform their duty. In the early days of February the feeding of the army became a pressing problem, and still the Omsk Ministers remained silent. On February 10 Pastrokoff received an imperative order to appear at General Hepoff's office. At 11 A.M. he arrived to find nine of the wealthiest citizens of Perm already collected. Looking out of the windows they saw a full company of Siberian Rifles surround the building with fixed bayonets. The general entered the room and sat at his table, they remained standing. Looking at, and *through*, each one separately, he delivered this cryptic speech : " Gentlemen, I have brought you here to tell you that out on the railway between you and your enemies lie the remains of our brave army ! They have little clothes, but plenty of wood, so their fires may prevent their bodies from being frozen, but ten days from now there will be no food, and unless food can be secured, nothing can prevent their dispersal or starvation. I have determined that they shall neither disperse nor starve. The Omsk Ministers have forgotten us, the Supreme Governor has given his orders, but these paltry people who ought to assist him do nothing. We must do their work ourselves." Reading down a list of the necessities of his army he said : "You gentlemen will produce these things within ten days. If on February 21 these supplies are not to hand, that will be the end of everything so far as you ten gentlemen are concerned."

" He allowed no discussion," said M. Pastrokoff, " and if he had we should have been discussing it now, and the Terrorists would have re-occupied Perm. I returned home and felt cold in the feet. I had a guard of fifteen men placed on my person, the others the same. I knew that some of my companions in distress were muddlers, but sent for my friend —— and drew our plans for carrying out the general's orders. We were greatly helped in this determination by witnessing the execution of a company and platoon commander of one of our regiments under General Hepoff's orders for having allowed thirty men of their company to desert to the enemy during an affair of outposts. We saw we had to deal with a man who never went back on his word."

On February 18 the general sent his aide-de-camp to inform the ten that it would be necessary for them to put their affairs in order as they would be taken to the front for execution, so that the starving soldiers might know their immediate chiefs were not responsible for the condition of the army. M.

With the "Die-Hards" in Siberia

Pastrokoff was able to prove the things were on the way, and only the disorganised condition of the railway made it necessary to ask for a few days' grace. The general granted four days, at the end of which the goods were delivered as per instructions. " What did the general then do? " I asked. " When his soldiers were fed he burst into my house and kissed me, and would have gone on his knees if I would have allowed him. He has been here several times since, and we have become great friends. He is a true Russian! " added Pastrokoff proudly.

We returned to Ekaterinburg on April 29, and were surprised to find that General Knox and the Headquarters Staff had removed from Omsk and taken up position there. The Hampshires were about to move up; barrack and other accommodation had already been secured. The first echelon arrived the following morning. An Anglo-Russian brigade of infantry was in course of formation and seemed likely to prove a great success. It offered employment for the numerous officers and N.C.O.s who had arrived and for whom no proper place for work had so far been provided. It was truly a stroke of genius for our War Office to flood us with officers and men as instructors for the new Russian army, scarcely one of whom could speak a word of Russian! I feel sure the Russians and ourselves will get on well together, we are so much alike. Omsk and Whitehall are true to type; they each first exhaust the possibility of error, and when no wrong course is left, the right road becomes quite easy. The only difference is in the motive. Ours is mostly because social influence

In European Russia

is always on the side of educated mediocrity, and theirs because self, coupled with corruption, is their natural incentive to all exertion. We have a different standard; all our theories of Government preclude the possibility of hidden personal advantage in the transaction of State business. The Russian view is that no competent official could be expected to conduct business transactions for the State unless he personally gains some advantage. If an official neglected a private opportunity so obvious, it would justify the suspicion that his scruples would make him unequal to the proper protection of the State. In other words, the official who is poor at the end of a decent term of office never should have been trusted with the interests of the community. It is strange to hear them catalogue the proved cases of corruption amongst officials of other countries. They never forget a case of this kind no matter in which country it occurred. They argue that they are no worse than others, forgetting that these exceptions only prove the rule, whereas in Russia the honest official is rather the exception. After all, public opinion decides the standard of conduct adopted by a country. Morals change with time, also with countries and peoples. A harem would be a nuisance in London, but stands as a sign of Allah's blessing in Constantinople.

I returned to Omsk on May 3 to find that the snow and ice had given place to a storm of dust which crept through every crevice of one's habitation and flavoured everything with dirt and grit. It was, if anything, worse than a sandstorm in the Sudan. The Sudan type is fairly clean, but this Omsk variety

With the "Die-Hards" in Siberia

is a cloud of atomic filth which carries with it every known quality of pollution and several that are quite unknown. I don't remember being able to smell a Sudan storm, but this monstrous production stank worse than a by-election missile. The service of a British soldier on these special trips is not exactly a sinecure. The people at home who pay can be sure their money is well earned before Tommy gets it. The south wind sweeps up from Mongolia and Turkestan, and while it brings warmth to our frozen bones its blessing becomes a bit mixed with other things before we get them. I only mention it, not to complain! We never do in war-time!

A special dispatch from London arrived on May 5 which delayed my starting for Vladivostok. If the object at which it aimed could have been secured it would have been a beam of light upon a very sombre subject. I had a lengthy conference with General Knox upon my tour to the Urals and the facts gathered as to the mineral and productive resources of the districts through which I had passed. The London dispatch also occupied our attention, and as the Supreme Governor had fixed the next day for my final farewell interview with himself, the possible course of our conversation was also considered. It was arranged that my journey to "Vlady" should be delayed until the matter referred to in the dispatch had been dealt with in accordance with instructions.

My audience with the Supreme Governor was very cordial, and he especially thanked me for the help I had rendered himself and Russia in the dark days of

In European Russia

November and December, 1918. He expressed the opinion that my mission to the workmen had been a great success, and was the first piece of definite work so far accomplished in the reconstruction and resurrection of the Russian State. He pointed out that his own labours were devoted to the one object of restoring order to the country, but that this work could only be performed by a powerful army. England had rendered him all help possible, but still the military problem engrossed all his thoughts and precluded his taking active part in the work of social reconstruction. He thought his Ministers and other assistants would have been able to help in it, but he had been sadly mistaken, and his experience had taught him that it was necessary to learn everything himself and therefore he was all the more grateful for my assistance. We took tea together, during which he informed me that he was about to start for the front to arrange for a further push along the northern line towards Vatka in the direction of Petrograd, with the chance of forming a junction with the forces at Archangel, and if General Knox would consent he wished me to remain at Omsk until he returned. General Knox placed the London dispatch before the Supreme Governor, and I remained to assist in settling its details.

On May 7 the Chief of the British Mission, Major-General Knox, asked me to assist him in drafting the reply to the London dispatch. The heads having been agreed to by the Supreme Governor, it was necessary to consult with the Minister who assisted him with his foreign affairs.

With the " Die-Hards " in Siberia

He is distinguished by a sort of cleverness which borders very closely to cunning. In a few years he will probably make a very able diplomat of the old type, but whether that is the sort of equipment which will serve under the new order, now in the throes of birth, remains to be seen. He is Republican, having lived long in America, and honestly believes that Russia must be directed in her orientation towards Republican countries rather than to the evidently permanently and exclusively Monarchist country, England. There I think I know more of his Russian fellow-countrymen and better understand their character and sentiments than he! But he is very young, very able, and his name is Sukin, and he has time to learn.

In accordance with the wish of the Governor, the dispatch and draft were shown to him, and a few hours later, while dining with a Cossack general, I was asked if I knew anything about a dispatch from London that was making a great stir amongst the members of the French and American Missions. I answered that being a regimental officer, not attached to the English Mission, dispatches were not my business, though as a rule if important dispatches arrived, I heard about them; I had heard of no dispatch which could upset the French or American Missions.

I informed Consul Hodgson, who was representing the High Commissioner in his absence, of this, and it was decided to hurry on with the construction and completion of the draft. It was completed in its final shape by General Knox and myself in his train

In European Russia

at the Omsk Vatka in front of the Russian Staffka, 9.30 A.M., May 9, 1919.

Much of this Russian "Bill of Rights" had to be pushed down the throats of the Russian official elements. The Supreme Governor never wavered over a single point; his large democratic sympathies were satisfied by his signature to what he hoped would be the foundation of Russian liberty. How fortunate for Russia that she had such a man to call upon in her hour of need! No matter what the final result of his efforts may be, whether success or defeat, his was the mind and personality that enabled this great people to bridge what looked like an impossible gulf and turn their faces to the sun.

How fortunate it was that at this critical hour in Russian history England was represented by Major-General Knox! I had never heard of him till I went to Siberia, yet in him we have a man combining the courage of the soldier with the higher qualities of a statesman, ready made for the special business in hand. The British Empire doubtless, like Topsy, "growed"! It is more an exhibition of race luck than genius. The way in which we occasionally drop the right man in the right place is not an act of Government so much as a stroke of chance. We make awful bloomers in these matters sometimes, but in this case our luck stood by us to some purpose. More than once, when the timidity of the " Politicals " had almost destroyed Russian faith in our honesty of purpose, the robust honesty of his personality turned the scale in our favour. Every Russian trusts him, except those who have forgotten they are Russians. They hate him. That is the real certificate of his worth. I can quite understand the fear of some Labour elements at home that our presence in Siberia may be used by reactionaries to re-establish the old régime. Had I been at home I might have had the same feeling. But I was there, and knew that it was our very presence which made that for the moment impossible. The excesses of the Bolsheviks made the people, both peasant and workman, hanker after the comparative security of the Tsars. The reactionary elements would have been only too pleased to see our backs; our presence was a safeguard against the absolutism for which some of them scheme. The weariness of the peasantry and workmen with revolutionary disorder gave the opportunity to reaction to establish another absolutism which was only restrained by outside influence. Major-General Knox does not write polished dispatches upon army movements under his command, but he perhaps performed greater service to humanity and democracy by his patient and efficient handling on the spot of one of the great world problems.

ADMIRAL KOLTCHAK.

CHAPTER XX

MAKING AN ATAMAN

GENERAL EVAN POOTENSEIFF arranged a parade of the 2nd Siberian Cossack Regiment outside Omsk on May 14 to say "Good-bye" to the "Anglisky Polkovnika," his officers and soldiers. Needless to say, we were all there, and it was an occasion that will be remembered by all who had the honour to be present. Those who look upon the Cossacks as a sort of untrained irregular cavalry had better revise their ideas at once, for fear of further future miscalculations. The evolutions of this force in every branch of cavalry work are simply superb. The Cossack control of his horse, either singly or in combination, is not approached by any army in the world. The parade was under the immediate command of the Assistant Ataman, Colonel Bezovsky, and the wonderful display of horsemanship was loudly applauded by the English Tommies, who were the most interested spectators.

The parade over, the officers adjourned to an extremely artistic Kirghis tent pitched on a treeless plain, where lunch was served; but the viands were left untouched until the toast of "His Britannic Majesty" had been drunk in good Tsaristic vodka. Then it became a real military fraternisation. Officers inside, soldiers out. No civilian was allowed to approach within three versts, except the old Kirghis chief who, dressed in his picturesque native dress, had travelled over fifty versts to attend the function of making an English Ataman. The band of the Cossack regiment tried valiantly to enliven the proceedings with music, but the English marching choruses soon silenced all opposition. Then the Cossack commander called his men around, and giving time with his cowhide thong, led them through some of the most weird Cossack war songs it is possible to imagine. The difference in our mentality was never so well illustrated as in the songs of the two people. Ours were lively, happy, and full of frolic and fun; theirs were slow, sad wails, which can only come from the heart of a long troubled people. The songs of Ermak Tinothavitch, the conqueror of Siberia, were fierce and martial, but the strain of tragedy ran through them all.

Then the Cossacks placed their commander upon two swords and tossed him while singing the song of Stenkarazin, the robber chief, and at the end drew their swords and demanded toll, which took the form of five bottles extra. I was then admitted to the fraternity and presented with the Ataman's badge, and after due ceremony with a Cossack sword, by the regiment, admitted to their circle. I went through the sword tossing, and gained freedom for 100 roubles; and here my narrative of the making of a Cossack had better end. Sufficient to say I never met a freer-hearted set of men in my travels round the world than these dreadful guardians of the Tsars, and if in course of time I get tired of England, I shall claim my kinship with these freemen of forest and plain. These men so love liberty that not even the Tsars dared interfere with their rights.

CHAPTER XXI

HOMEWARD BOUND

On May 17 Omsk was excluded from the Vatka (station), and by this indirect means became aware that the Supreme Governor was returning from the front. The Cossack Guard lined up outside, while detachments of Russian infantry in English uniform occupied the platform. The Russian Tommies looked quite smart, and except for their long, narrow, triangular bayonets, might easily have been mistaken for English troops. While awaiting the train, General Knox informed me that two of our proposals, " Women's suffrage " and " Universal education," had been cut out by the reactionaries. Why are the churches of the world so hostile to the popular education of the people? The Church is quite prepared to allow the people to receive educational instruction if controlled by the priests. It prefers to leave them in ignorance and the easy prey of Bolshevik charlatanism rather than allow free play for intelligent thinking. Women's suffrage was opposed by quite a different set of men, mostly those who make enormous display of deference to drawing-room ladies, and look upon us Englishmen as wanting in gallantry because we do not kiss every feminine hand we shake. On the whole I think it is good to have pushed them ahead so far. Measured by Russian standards, it amounts to a revolution in ideas of government. The great thing just now is to fix some point beyond which the pendulum shall not be allowed to swing towards reaction. The workmen are sick of strife and would gladly go straight back to the old régime as an easy way of escape from Bolshevism. This is the danger from which English diplomacy has tried, and is trying, to guard the Russian people if possible.

Thus, having finished my work at Omsk, I asked that arrangements might be made as quickly as possible to transport my escort and myself to Vladivostok. The arrangements were completed by May 21, when I announced myself ready to begin the first stage of my journey homeward. The Supreme Governor surprised me by proposing to visit me in my carriage at the Vatka to say "Good-bye." At 7 P.M. he came, attended by his aide-de-camp; he was very gracious in his thanks for my services to the Russian people. He said my voice, presence and influence had aroused the better elements to throw off the feeling of despair which had so universally settled upon them. He did not presume to calculate the good I had done, though none appreciated it better than himself, since we had been thrown by circumstances into personal contact with each other. Without attempting to form an estimate of his character, I considered his visit and words the act of a gentleman, and as such I appreciated it.

I could but recall the last time he visited me in

those dark, doubtful days of November, when I, who had no thought or place in my make-up for the word " Dictator," suddenly found myself in the presence of him who had that moment assumed such a position, and what was more serious for me, found myself forced on my own authority, unaided by one word of warning or counsel from others, instantly to decide not only my own attitude but also, to some extent, that of my country to this last act in the drama of a people grown desperate. Once having given my promise to help, he never found that help withheld at critical moments later. The British forces were few, but they were disciplined and knew their own mind, and this was what every other party, both Russian and Allied, lacked. Every Allied force had its " Politicals " at hand, and therefore were powerless for any purpose. The Fates had sent ours to Vladivostok, 5,000 versts east, at the very moment when their presence and general political policy would have paralysed correct military action. The month which intervened before they could exert direct influence upon the situation enabled us to consolidate the new orientation. The greater part of this time we were " in the air," having cut our own communications, and no countermanding orders could interrupt or confuse the nerve centre. At first the " Politicals " were inclined to be angry, but with such a tower of strength as General Knox in support they soon came to look upon the proceedings as a *fait accompli*. Later they confessed that their absence at the supreme moment was the act of a wise Providence. The very nature of their business (had they

Homeward Bound

been present) would have created delays and difficulties that might have proved fatal to success.

Except for some quaint fetish about the necessity for maintaining the usual diplomatic forms, there is no necessity for delay in emergencies of this description. If an ordinarily intelligent Englishman, with a fair knowledge of English history and a grasp of the traditions and mentality of his countrymen, cannot carry on, how are people miles away, with no opportunity to visualise the actual situation, to instruct him? Diplomatic methods and forms are all right for leisurely negotiations, but are useless in urgent and dangerous occasions. If my work fails, as even now it may, I shall be subject to severe criticism; but I shall get that even if it succeeds, so ,what does it matter so long as in my own mind I did the best in the circumstances?

My journey east was broken at Krasnoyarsk to enable me to interview the new commander, General Rosanoff, who had taken in hand the suppression of the revolt of the Lettish peasants north of the railway. South of the line all hostile elements had been dispersed. The line cut through the centre of the Bolshevik field of operations. The Czechs guarded the actual railway, and while they prevented large forces from moving across it, they took but little trouble to prevent miscreants from tampering with the rails, as was evidenced by the scores of derailed trains in all stages of destruction strewn along the track. This naturally involved great material loss and, what was still worse, a huge toll of innocent human life. One train, a fast passenger, accounted for two hundred women and children, besides uncounted men. Fairly large Russian forces were now placed at General Rosanoff's disposal, and by a wide turning movement from Krasnoyarsk in a north-easterly direction, and with a large cavalry force operating towards the north-west from Irkutsk, the whole gang would, it was hoped, be herded towards the centre, and a few weeks would probably liquidate the whole disturbance. The Krasnoyarsk and the Ussurie movements of the Bolsheviks were under the direction of able officers appointed by the Red Guard Headquarters at Moscow, with whom they were in constant communication.

Passing Irkutsk, we again struck the Baikal—looking more glorious than before. The warm south-west winds had cleared the snow from the western hills and thawed the ice from that half of the sea. The other half was still ice-bound. In the morning sunshine the snow-covered mountains in the east pierced the heavens with the radiance of eternal day. The disappearance of the sun only adds to their beauty; they alone seem to know no night. As we travelled round under the shadow of these giants the temperature fell many degrees below zero, and the cold from the water penetrated the carriages, necessitating fires and warm furs, in spite of the June sunshine.

I had received intimation that it would be of service to the Omsk Government if I would call upon Colonel Semianoff and use my good offices and my newly-conferred honour as a Siberian Cossack Ataman to recall this erring son of Muscovy to the service of the State. I knew that British pressure had been applied to persuade the Japanese to cease their financial and moral support—both open and secret—to this redoubtable opponent of the Russian Government, and it was rumoured that British wishes had at last been complied with. It was common knowledge that the illegal floggings, murders, and robberies committed under the alleged authority of Colonel Semianoff would not have remained unpunished a day if he had not been under the protection of one of the most numerously represented Allied forces. Whatever faults may be alleged against Admiral Koltchak, cruelty or injustice cannot be included among them. I well remember his fury when it was reported to him that some eighty workmen had been illegally flogged by Semianoff's soldiers at Chita. His poor dilapidated reserves were ordered to move at once to their protection. Semianoff prepared his armoured trains and troops to receive them, but the same Allied Power which fed, clothed, and armed his troops kept at bay those who were ordered to avenge the wrongs of the Russian workmen.

On another occasion I remember Admiral Koltchack's almost hopeless despair when some truculent officers has used their weapons and badges of rank to secure the persons of some Bolshevik prisoners, and anticipating the decision of the court about to try them, shot them in cold blood. He at once executed the officers and men who handed them over, as well as such of those who took part in the conspiracy, even though they claimed to be merely the avengers of

With the " Die-Hards " in Siberia

their own murdered families. Stern, impartial justice
is part and parcel of this remarkable man's character.
It was this very trait which made Semianoff and the
Supreme Governor natural enemies.

The day that I arrived at Chita it was officially
announced that Semianoff had made his submission
to the authority of Koltchak, and had accepted an
appointment in the Russian Army. My task therefore changed its character; the proposed admonish-
ment became a congratulation in a very frank and
friendly half-hour's interview, the colonel returning
the visit to my carriage later. Colonel Semianoff is
one of the most striking personalities I have met
in Russia; a man of medium height, with square
broad shoulders, an enormous head, the size of which
is greatly enhanced by the flat, Mongol face, from
which gleam two clear, brilliant eyes that rather
belong to an animal than a man. The whole pose
of the man is at first suspicious, alert, determined,
like a tiger ready to spring, to rend and tear, but
in repose the change is remarkable, and with a quiet
smile upon the brown face the body relaxes. Colonel
Semianoff is a very pleasant personality. His great
physical strength has caused the Japanese to name
him " Samurai," or " Brave Knight of the Field,"
and I think that is a good description of his character.
Relentless and brave, kindness nevertheless finds a
part in his make-up. The princes of Mongolia have
asked him to become their emperor, and should he
choose this path a whirlwind will pass over the neigh-
bouring lands. Perhaps underneath he is, after all,
a good Russian—time will tell. If his conversion is

real he will add a tower of strength to the Russian fighting forces.

At Harbin I heard a full explanation of the reason for the Mongolians approaching Semianoff to become their emperor. Mongolia previous to the Revolution was considered as under a loose sort of Russian protection. Since the break-up of the Russian Empire the Japanese have cast longing eyes upon this extensive country, which is supposed to belong to both Russia and China but in reality it belongs to neither. The Japanese have roamed all over the country during these last two years, and have spent time and money lavishly in propaganda. They first tried to orientate the Mongol mind towards a direct connection with themselves, but their avarice and conceit offend all the people with whom they come into contact. This direct method of getting control of Mongolia had therefore to be abandoned in favour of a round-about but more dangerous policy. Colonel Semianoff is only half Russian, his mother being a Mongolian woman of high birth. He speaks Mongolian perfectly, and the Mongolians claim him for their own. Semianoff admitted to me personally that he had been subsidised all through by Japan. It was the Japanese who called the Mongolian princes together and prevailed upon them to offer Semianoff the title of Emperor of Mongolia. He had other fish to fry, however, but when his other schemes fail, as I think they must, he will be quite ready to play the Japanese game in Mongolia as faithfully as he did in Siberia. Semianoff will be the puppet, but Japan will pull the strings; that at least is their hope and belief.

With the "Die-Hards" in Siberia

About thirty versts west of Manchuli our train
was stopped by a red flag, and a railway workman
informed us of a raid upon a homestead by the side
of the railway, the robbers having decamped two
hours before our arrival. The father had two bullets
through his chest and one through the right side of
his neck, and had crawled a distance of over a verst
to give information. He was taken up on our train,
and we went forward to the scene of the tragedy.
In the small wooden house, covered with loose
feathers, lay the dead body of the mother with her
unborn baby, near by lay a girl of about ten with
her head terribly wounded. In an outhouse was the
body of their Chinese boy. My hospital orderly
rendered what aid was possible to the girl, who was
carried by Madame Frank to my carriage for con-
veyance to the hospital at Manchuli. A civilian
doctor declared both cases hopeless, and the depo-
sitions of the man were taken. Briefly thus:

When the Bolsheviks first occupied Manchuli a
railway workman of anarchist tendencies was
appointed Soviet Commissar of the district. Afterwards, when the Bolshevik power was destroyed and
their forces were driven off the railway, the Bolshevik
bands took to the forest, some engaging in running
contraband over the Chinese frontier, others forming
themselves into bands who not only robbed the
isolated peasantry, but forced young men to join
them, and afterwards levied toll upon large villages
and small towns. About three in the morning this
Bolshevik Commissar knocked at the cottage door
and asked the father to let him come in, as he was

Homeward Bound

very tired, having had a long journey with contraband. Believing him to be alone, the man opened the
door. The room was immediately filled with armed
men, who demanded his savings or his life. The
commissar, from his knowledge of such matters,
believing his savings to be in the feather pillow,
ripped it open and found 4,600 roubles. Having
collected all the other small articles of value in the
house, these innocent children of the Revolution held
consultation on the necessity of killing everybody
who knew them to be Bolsheviks, so that the crime
should be cast upon the Chinese robber gangs who
occasionally raid Russian territory. This important
point in the regeneration of Russia settled, they shot
the man in the chest, the bullet coming out by the
shoulder-blade. The wife, begging for the life of
her husband, was bayoneted, and the aroused Chinese
workman was dispatched with a rifle. Then these
harmless idealists proceeded to depart. So far they
had not touched the girl, but the father, on regaining
consciousness, heard the closed door open again, saw
the leader of the " comrades " re-enter and pick up
a small axe near the fire, with which he proceeded
to smash the head of the child. Nature in its terrible
revolt gave the father the power to raise himself
slightly from the floor in a vain effort to grapple with
this representative of the new régime. The commissar shouted : " What, still alive ! " and fired two more
point-blank shots at the prostrate man.

It was entirely due to the tenacity of the father
that the object of the killing was frustrated and the
identification of the scoundrels with the Bolshevik

commanders operating in this neighbourhood completed. I had no time to pick up the trail and punish the murderers. What sort of punishment the Tommies would have decided as necessary to fit the crime is better imagined than described!

It was June when we passed over the Hinghan range, a series of sand mountains of great extent which form the breeding-ground for numerous herds of horses who spread themselves over the slopes and plains and sometimes endanger the safety of the railway. Snow was falling in clouds, and banked itself against the rails and telegraphs in a surprising manner considering the time of the year. The summer of this wild region lasts about two months—July and August—during which time the sand becomes hot, and travelling is not comfortable. After crossing the summit the plains fell gradually away, enabling the trains to move with great rapidity, and in less than two days we struck Harbin, and donned our topees and tropical clothes.

Harbin is the centre of Chinese and Russian political and financial intrigue. Other races take a fair hand in the business, but the predominance must be conceded to these two. There is some sort of national feeling amongst the worst type of Russian speculator, but none amongst the Chinese. The Harbin Chinaman is perfectly denationalised, and ought, therefore, according to some standards of political reckonings, to be the most ideal citizen in the world; but the world who knows him hopes that for ever he may be exclusively confined to Harbin. I had a long conversation with General Ghondati, one of the most level-headed living statesmen of the old régime. All his hopes are centred on the success of Admiral Koltchak in his efforts to secure order to enable the National Assembly to consider the question of a Constitutional Monarchy on England's pattern to be established at Moscow. If this cannot be, he fears Russia's travail will last longer and may be fatal to her existence. He was not himself opposed to a Federal Republic, but was certain that without a head the undisciplined semi-oriental elements would never accept the abolition of absolutism as final. The Russian people have it in their bones to obey a leader; their warlike nature precludes the possibility of their continued loyalty to a junta, however able. A crown on top, with a parliament to control and direct, would be the happiest solution of Russia's present difficulties. He summed his theory up in these words: " A properly elected parliament to make the law and rule, but there must be a monarch to issue its orders."

Though this is the expressed opinion of what the Bolshevik would term one of the " old régime," it is nevertheless the openly-expressed opinion of the sensible leaders of every class of Russian society except two—the Bolsheviks at one end, and the Absolutists at the other. More than once already these two extremes have come close together to frustrate the possibility of a compromise on constitutional lines. They openly declare that, unless power is given to either one or the other, they would prefer that the present anarchy should continue. It is not the first time in revolutionary history that

With the " Die-Hards" in Siberia

the adherents of autocracy (Royalist and otherwise) have preferred the ruin of their country rather than lose their own personal power.

Ghondati is a clear-headed patriot, and I am surprised that his counsel has not been sought for in this supreme moment of his country's history. His ideas relating to recognition by the Powers were rather remarkable. He did not think that any country could give help to Russia without either asking for conditions or being suspected of doing so. The only exception was England. The reason England is not suspected is that her Empire is so vast and varied in character that she has all the raw material for her trade and all the space she requires for her surplus population. Her help, unlike that of any other State so far, has been unselfish and unconditional. Ghondati quite saw that "this fact was producing a steady and permanent orientation of Russian opinion towards England, which, if cultivated by British statesmanship, would eventually give my country everything she required, while those whose help was always surrounded with conditions would have great difficulty to retain the advantages they secured only under the pressure of circumstances."

CHAPTER XXII

AMERICAN POLICY AND ITS RESULTS

AT Nikolsk my train was stopped as the No. 4 Post train from Vladivostok had been wrecked by Bolsheviks, a startling situation considering that eleven months previously the whole power of Bolshevism had been destroyed in these maritime provinces. The station commandant was an old friend, who had given me his own private official carriage at the time when our little yellow brother had decided to lower the prestige of his white Ally in Eastern eyes by making British officers travel in cattle-trucks. He came into my car and began to explain how the cross-purposes of the American and Japanese forces were producing a state of uncertainty and disorder as bad, if not worse, than existed under the Bolshevik régime. Our conversation was cut short by the receipt of a telegram from the station-master at Kraevesk. It was to the effect that he was using his own line from his house, because a few minutes previously a detachment of the Red Guard had entered the station and, in the presence of the American soldiers who were guarding the railway, had placed himself and his staff under arrest and taken possession of the station; that the Reds had sent a message to Shmakovka ordering all Russian railway officials and staff to leave their posts, as the

With the "Die-Hards" in Siberia

Bolshevik army, with the sanction of the American forces, was about to take over the line. The Red Guard officer in proof of his order stated "that fifteen American soldiers are now standing in the room from which I am sending this message." Having issued these orders in the presence of the Americans, they had removed the telegraph and telephone apparatus, and the station-master wished to know what he was to do and whether any help could be sent him. Imagine my utter astonishment at this message, containing, as it undoubtedly did, evidence of co-operation and understanding between the Bolshevik forces and one of our Allies.

In one of my numerous interviews with Admiral Koltchak at Omsk he had made some very serious statements regarding the American policy in the Far East, which he feared would result in reproducing the previous state of disorder. I assured him that the policy of the Allies was to resist disorder and support order, and that I could not believe America had come to Siberia to make his task more difficult, but to help him in every reasonable way. He agreed that such was the intention of the American people, but he feared that the American command was being used for quite other purposes. His officers had informed him that out of sixty liaison officers and translators with American Headquarters over fifty were Russian Jews or the relatives of Russian Jews; some had been exiled from Russia for political and other offences, and had returned as American citizens, capable of influencing American policy in a direction contrary to that desired by the American people. I assured him that this could not be, and that his people might themselves in this matter be under the influence of a near Eastern neighbour not friendly to American interference in Eastern affairs, and that under this influence they might greatly magnify the danger. My words seemed to ease the admiral's mind, but he regretfully replied that the reports were so voluminous and categorical in character that he thought I, as a representative of the people of England, as well as an officer of His Majesty's Army, ought to be made acquainted with the situation.

This matter had almost disappeared from my mind, but the message from the station-master at Kraevesk revived it with the vividness of a sudden blow. I at once determined to make myself acquainted as far as possible with the policy of the American commanders, and with this object in view I interviewed many American officers and soldiers. I found that both officers and men were most anxious to render all the help possible to maintain Koltchak's authority and crush disorder in the Far East, and, as they put it, "justify their presence in Siberia." Many felt that at the time they were only helping the Bolsheviks to recover their lost hold upon the people by providing neutral territory for Bolshevik propaganda; that when they arrived in the country in August, 1918, the English, Czechs, and Japanese, with the aid of such Russian units as then existed, had reduced the maritime provinces to order, but that their own efforts had produced a state of affairs similar to, if not worse than, those which existed during the actual Bolshevik occupation. I learnt from these American troops that their officers and officials, from General Graves downwards, had been in actual correspondence with Red Guard officers, and that more than one understanding had been arrived at between them ; that for a time the ordinary American soldiers thought the understanding between the two forces was so general and friendly in character that no further hostile acts were to be contemplated between them. It was true that this wrecking of trains and attacks on the line guarded by American soldiers made things look serious, but they felt sure that the confidence existing between the American and Red Guard Headquarters was so well established that these acts of brigandage could only be due to some misunderstanding. The Kraevesk affair appeared to be only a symptom of a much wider policy, and not the foolish act of a negligent subordinate officer.

Following up my inquiries there fell into my hands a letter, dated May 24, from the American officer (Captain ——) commanding the American forces at Svagena, addressed to the officer commanding the Red Guard operating in that district. The American officer addressed the Red Guard commandant as a recognised officer of equal military standing. The American officer complained that after a recent fraternisation of the two forces which had taken place in accordance with previous arrangements near the " wood mill," on the departure of the Red troops he received reports that the Red Guard officer had ordered the destruction of certain

American Policy and its Results

machinery at the mill, and had also torn up two sections of the line at points east and west of the station at Svagena. The American captain enumerated other accusations against the Red Guard, such as threats to bayonet certain orderly disposed people who would not join the Bolshevik army, and warned the Red Commissar that these acts were contrary to the *agreement* entered into by the chiefs of the American and Red forces, and if such acts were repeated he would take steps to punish those who committed such breaches of *their joint understanding*.

I think this letter from the American officer at Svagena is positive proof of some local or general understanding between the American authorities and the Red army operating in the maritime provinces, and further, that this understanding had existed for many months; that it was this understanding which prevented the American forces joining in the combined Allied expedition to relieve the besieged Russian garrison in the Suchan district; that under this American-Bolshevik agreement the small scattered Red Guard bands who were dispersed by the Allies at the battle of Dukoveskoie in August, have collected together and formed definite military units. In other words, that the American policy, unconsciously or otherwise, has produced a state of indecision amongst the Allies, and unrest and anarchy amongst the population of the Transbaikal and Ussurie Provinces, which may prove disastrous to the rapid establishment of order in Russia.

There are other indications that the presence of the American forces in Siberia has been used by somebody for purposes not purely American. The business of the American command is to secure order in those districts which have been placed under its control by the Council of Allied Commanders. There is another self-evident and obvious duty, namely, to shape their conduct in such manner as to create friendly relations with such elements of Russian authority and order as are gradually appearing here and there, under the influence of the Supreme Governor, and also provide as little space and opportunity as possible for the collection and reorganisation of the elements of disorder. The policy of the American command, quite unintentionally perhaps, has been quite the reverse. Their policy has resulted in turning every Russian authority against them, or, where this has not happened, they have themselves turned against Russian authority. They have prepared plans and created opportunities for the reorganisation of the forces of disorder which, if it does not actually create a serious situation for themselves, will do so for those Allies who are trying to bring order out of chaos. The reduction of the whole country to order, to enable it to decide its own future form of Government, is as much an American as a British object. That some sinister underground influence has deflected American policy from this straight and honest course is quite obvious.

Contrary to general Allied opinion, the American command declared a neutral zone in the Suchan district. Armed operations by Russian, i.e. Admiral Koltchak's or Red Guard forces, were prohibited within this zone. Lenin and Trotsky's officers

American Policy and its Results

jumped at this order and at once began to collect their scattered forces together. Within three weeks they raised their Bolshevik flag on their own head-quarters, under the protection of the flag of the United States. From this neutral American zone the Bolsheviks organised their forces for attacking the Japanese on the Amur, for destroying British and other supply trains on the Ussurie Railway, and finally exchanged shots with the Russian sentries near Vladivostok itself, always bolting back to the American zone when attacked by the forces of the Supreme Governor.

The other Allies and the Russians having got the measure of this neutral zone business, naturally took steps to protect their men and property, and for a time the operations of this very energetic Lenin officer were confined to robbing and destroying a few isolated villages in the maritime provinces; but the utter absurdity of American policy was at last brought home to the Americans themselves. The Red Guard commandant, chafing under the restrictions imposed upon him by the Russian and Japanese forces (in which the British also joined when Captain Edwards could get near with his good ship *Kent*), decided to attack the unsuspecting Americans themselves. The Red Guard were very clever in their operations. The American troops were guarding the Vladivostok-Suchan Railway; the neutral zone was situated at the extreme end of the line. If the Red Guard had attacked the end near the zone their tactics would have been discovered at once. They therefore usually marched out from the American zone, made a detour through villages and forest, and struck the railway at a point as far distant as possible. Destroying a bit of line—perhaps, if they had good luck, burning a bridge—they usually exchanged a few shots with the American troops, and if pressed, marched back to the zone under the protection of a section of the very forces they had been raiding. The American command naturally became more vigilant on the distant sections of the line, and this forced the Bolsheviks to operate nearer and nearer the protected zone; but in the meantime they managed to kill several Russian soldiers, wound a few Americans, and destroy five different sections of the railway. Then they operated too near the zone, and the American troops pressed them straight into their own zone, where, to add insult to injury, they claimed that in accordance with the American proclamation they could not be molested as military operations were prohibited within the zone!

Instead of proceeding to root out this nest of pirates, someone suggested that a more comprehensive and binding arrangement was necessary between the American and Red Guard forces, to prevent such regrettable occurrences in future. It was common talk that a conference between the Red Guard commander and General Graves, the American G.O.C., was actually arranged, but was dropped when the Supreme Governor's representative in the Far East declared to General Graves personally that his proposed conference with the enemies of the Russian Government would be considered as a hostile act. The breaking off of these negotiations caused great annoy-

American Policy and its Results

ance to the Soviet Government at Moscow, and they ordered their commissars in Ussurie to use the forces which had been organised under American protection to attack their protectors, which they at once proceeded to do. This doubtless altered the relationship of these two parties, though the chances are that the powerful influence which forced the American commanders into this ill-fated policy will be powerful enough to prevent an open American declaration against the Reds in the Far East.

It is well at this stage to estimate the effect this American muddle has had, and will continue to exert, upon the effort of the Allies to secure some sort of order in the Russian Empire, and upon the position of the Americans themselves in their future relations with the Russian people. The American troops were spread over the whole province from Vladivostok to Nevsniudinsk, a point just east of the Sea of Baikal. They were almost entirely confined to the railway, but in this country the railway is the centre and heart of all things. American policy at Vladivostok applied to the whole of this area, which is really the Transbaikal provinces, or all Siberia east of Baikal. In the early days of September, 1918, when I passed with my battalion towards Omsk, this immense area had been reduced to order by the efforts of the Allies, at the head of which I place the gallant Czechs. The American forces arrived too late to take part in the military operations, but began to settle down to the work of administration with energy and ability. The French moved forward after myself, and the Italian unit followed later, leaving the American and

With the "Die-Hards" in Siberia

Japanese, with such isolated local Russian forces as had called themselves into being, in absolute possession of Transbaikal Siberia. There was not a single band of Red Guards one thousand strong in the whole territory. After nine months of Allied occupation the Reds organised, largely under American protection, two divisions (so called) of from 5,000 to 7,000 men, and numerous subsidiary units of a few hundred, who murdered and robbed in every direction, and destroyed every semblance of order which the Supreme Governor and the Allies had with so much labour attempted to set up. Thus this huge province in a short time descended from comparative order to sporadic disorder, simply because America had no Russian policy of her own, and rejected that of her friends.

It was a major mistake of England and France to leave America and Japan cheek by jowl without a moderating influence, to wreck the good work they had accomplished in the Far East. The rivalries of these two Powers in this part of the world were well known and should have been provided for. It was too much to expect that they would forget their concession and trade rivalries in a disinterested effort to help Russia. States are not usually philanthropic organisations, these two least of all. The work has therefore to be largely done over again, either by us or by the Supreme Governor, Admiral Koltchak. Or the Allies, finding the task too great, may retire and allow this huge province, probably the wealthiest part of the world, to recede back to the barbarism of the Bolshevik.

CHAPTER XXIII

JAPANESE POLICY AND ITS RESULTS

THE lack of Allied cohesion produced by the defection of American policy from that of the European Powers may change completely the status and future of American enterprise in Siberia. America has transformed a friendly population into at least a suspicious, if not a hostile, one. Japan, on the other hand, has steadily pursued her special interests and taken full advantage of every American mistake, until she is now looked upon as the more important of the two.

The attitude of Japan to the Russian problem made a complete somersault in the course of the year August, 1918, to August, 1919. When Japan sent her 12th Division, under General Oie, to the Ussurie in 1918, she did so with a definite policy. Her ambitions were entirely territorial in character; they doubtless remain so. The line of her advance has, however, completely changed. In 1918 she had made up her mind that Germany was bound to win the war; that Russia was a conquered country; that any day she might be called upon to repudiate her English alliance and her Entente engagements, and assist Germany and her Bolshevik Allies in driving the Entente Powers from the eastern end of the Tsar's dominions. Provided Germany defeated the Allies on the Western front, as she confidently anticipated, this task was well within her power. So insignificant was the task assigned to her in this eventuality that she confidently expected the immediate surrender of such scattered Allied and American forces as would find themselves marooned in this back end of the world. Believing this to be the position, she acted accordingly, treating the Russians and the other Allied forces in the stupidly arrogant manner I have already described. With the *naïveté* of a young Eastern prodigy she not only made demands upon her Allies, but at the same time made definite proposals to such Russian authorities as retained a precarious control over the territory she had already assigned to herself. On landing her troops at Vladivostok she presented, through her proper diplomatic agents, to the commander of that province a set of proposals which would have placed her in control of the Russian maritime provinces. The Russian commander asked that these demands should be put in writing, and the Japanese agent, after some demur, agreed, on the understanding that the first demands should not be considered as final but only as an instalment of others to come. The first proposal was that Japan should advance the commander 150,000,000 roubles (old value) and the commander should sign an agreement giving Japan possession of the foreshore and fishing rights up to Kamchatka, a perpetual lease of the Engilsky mines, and the whole of the iron (less that belonging to the Allies) to be found in Vladivostok.

The Town Commander appears to have been

Japanese Policy and its Results

quite honest about the business, for in correspondence he pointed out that he was not the Government of Russia, neither could he sign the property or rights of Russia away in the manner suggested. The Japanese reply was simple and to the point : " Take our money and sign the agreement, and we will take the risks about the validity." The old Directorate, with Avkzentieff, Bolderoff & Co. standing sponsors for the Russian Convention, were supposed to control Russian affairs at this time. Directly the commandant refused to agree to the Japanese demands they transferred their claims to the old Directorate. The Directorate sent Evanoff Renoff to " Vlady " to conduct the negotiations, and I suppose to collect the money. When I was at " Vlady," in June, 1919, huge stores of iron were being collected, and some of it had already been shipped to Japan. Avkzentieff was exiled and Bolderoff was living in comfort and safety in Japan. These were the things that were above and could be seen ; what happened to the other part of the first instalment of Japanese proposals for " helping " Russia will doubtless be known later.

At the end of August, 1918, it was decided that until some sort of central authority to act as the organ of Government was set up, it was futile to hope for the return of orderly government. For this purpose the British went forward to Omsk and asked the Japanese to do likewise. The Japanese would not move, first because they wished to consolidate their power in the provinces nearest Japan, and secondly secure as many concessions as possible before America arrived on the scene. When America did arrive she still tarried to watch American operations. The British moved off into the unknown with a 5,000-mile line of unguarded communications; the Japanese, true to type, opened negotiations with the Directorate for the absolute possession of the railway to the Urals, and also asked what concessions she could expect to receive, territorial and mineral, as compensation for the use of her army for the Directorate's protection. A convention had just been signed, or was on the point of signature, between the Japanese and the Directorate, placing the entire railway under Japanese hands, when the Directorate fell. The first act of the Supreme Governor, Admiral Koltchak, was to inform the Japanese that the change in the Government involved a change in policy with regard to the advance of Japanese troops and the occupation of the railway. The Japanese protested, but the admiral stood firm.

This attitude of the Supreme Governor was a serious setback to Japanese policy, and they became alarmed for their position in the Far East should his authority extend in that direction; but it is not difficult as a rule to find tools for any kind of work in Russia. Ataman Semianoff had for some time been kept by the Japanese in reserve for such an occasion. His forces were ranged around Chita, and his influence and authority extended from the Manchurian border to Lake Baikal. On receiving intimation of the change in policy from Admiral Koltchak, the Japanese ordered Semianoff to repudiate the Supreme Governor's authority; they gave the same instructions to Kalmakoff, who occupied

Japanese Policy and its Results

a similar position on the Ussurie Railway and so placed an effective barrier between themselves, their Eastern concessions, and the Supreme Governor. The Supreme Governor ordered his Staff to clear these two mutineers off the line, but the Japanese Staff informed the Supreme Governor that these two Russian patriots and their forces were under the protection of Japan, and if necessary they would move the Japanese Army forward to their succour.

The successful resistance of Semenoff and Kalmakoff to the Omsk Government, backed up by the armed forces of one of the Allies, had a disastrous effect upon the situation throughout Siberia. If Semianoff and Kalmakoff could, with Allied help and encouragement, openly deride the Omsk Government's orders, then it was clear to the uninitiated that the Allies were hostile to the supreme Russian authority. If Semianoff and Kalmakoff can wage successful hired resistance to orderly government at the bidding of a foreign Power, why cannot we do so, to retain the land and property we have stolen and prevent the proper administration of justice for the crimes we have committed? It was intended as a deliberate attack upon authority and an incentive to the disorderly elements to continue the prevailing anarchy. A united, well organised Russia is not the kind of Russia Japan wishes to see established. If Japan is to succeed in her territorial ambitions in the Far East, Russia must be kept in a state of mental disorder and physical paralysis. Germany used the Russian love of conspiracy and intrigue to create disorder and destroy the Muscovite power; Japan intends, if possible, to continue that disorder for her own political reasons.

Directly it became known that Semianoff and Kalmakoff had set the Omsk Government at defiance, numerous other would-be Semenoffs came on the scene until the very residence of the Supreme Governor and his Headquarters Staff scarcely escaped attack, and it became necessary to show the British Tommy on the side of order. This was the position up till the early days of December, 1918.

Just about this time the fact that Germany was beaten began to take shape in the Japanese military mind, and the fact was hammered home by the terms of the Armistice. For some days the Japanese Mission at Omsk flatly refused to believe the cables; their national pride refused to admit that they had so far misunderstood the power of Britain and her Allies. It was a terrible awakening to the self-styled " Lords of the East " that all their schemes should be brought to nought, that British and American squadrons might be expected to cruise in the Sea of Japan, and perhaps hold the scales fair between her and her temporarily helpless neighbour. I do not suppose it will ever come to that, but such was her fear. From this time on, while the objects of Japan in Siberia were still the same, she pursued them by quite different methods.

The first sign of change was that Japanese soldiers were allowed to salute British officers and were no longer allowed to use the butts of their rifles on inoffensive Russian citizens. Their military trains no longer conveyed contraband goods to their com-

Japanese Policy and its Results

patriots who had *acquired* the Russian business houses in the main trading centres along the railway. The Staff no longer commandeered the best buildings in the towns for alleged military purposes and immediately sub-let them to private traders. Japan at once re-robed herself with the thin veil of Western morals and conduct which she had rapturously discarded in 1914. While Hun methods were in the ascendancy she adopted the worst of them as her own. She is in everything the imitator *par excellence,* and therefore apparently could not help herself.

The British and French mildly protested against the attitude of Japan towards Semianoff and Kalmakoff, but it was continued until the anarchy created threatened to frustrate every Allied effort. Not until the Peace Conference had disclosed the situation did a change in policy take place. From this time on the conduct of Japan (both civil and military) became absolutely correct. President Wilson brought forward his famous, but impossible, proposal that the different Russian belligerents should agree to an armistice and hold a conference on the Turkish " Isle of Dogs.'' If patriotism is the maintenance of such rules of human conduct and national life as will justify one man in killing another, then no Russian patriot could meet in friendly conference those who had destroyed and murdered their own country and people. Russia during the previous two years had shown that there could be no compromise between anarchy and order, or their several adherents. This was, however, the policy of America, and as such received the blessing of every representative, Jew

With the "Die-Hards" in Siberia

or Gentile, of the U.S.A. in Siberia. Japan saw a
kink in the American armour and took full advantage
of the chance to damage U.S.A. prestige. She
rallied Russian patriotism to her side by advising that
no notice be taken of this harebrained suggestion.
Japan's advice received the secret blessing of both
French and English who knew the situation, though
in our case we had to admit that the British Premier
had stood sponsor for this international monstrosity.
This gave Japanese diplomacy its first clear hold upon
Russian patriotism and enabled her to appear as a true
friend of orderly government.

American diplomacy in Russia had received its
first great shock, but with careful handling it was still
possible to recover the lost ground. With the utter
failure of the " Isle of Dogs " policy, Russian rage
quickly subsided and a normal condition soon returned. The Allies had received a salutary warning,
and most of them took the hint, but America continued on her debatable course. Having failed diplo-
matically to effect a compromise, she tried to force
her views by military means. The neutral zone
system of her commanders was the natural outcome
of President Wilson's proposal. The intention was
excellent, that the results would be disastrous was
never in doubt. It forced the American command to
adopt a sort of local recognition of the Red Army
within the zone, and enabled the Japanese to appear
as the sole friend of Russian order. The Japanese
were attacked by Red forces collected in these zones,
with American soldiers standing as idle spectators of
some of the most desperate affairs between Red and

Japanese Policy and its Results

Allied troops. Japan was entitled to reap the kudos such a situation brought to her side, while America could not expect to escape the severest censure.

Profiting by the blunders of her great antagonist, Japan managed in six months to recover all the ground she had lost while suffering under the illusion of a great Hun victory that was to give her the Lordship of the East. From a blustering bandit she has become a humble helper of her poor, sick, Russian neighbour. In which rôle she is most dangerous time will show. The world as a rule has little faith in sudden conversions.

This, then, was the situation in the Far East in June, 1919. As I was leaving Vladivostok I heard that the Red forces that had been organised in the American neutral zones had at last boldly attacked their protectors. If this was correct, it may be the reason why Admiral Koltchak was able to report their defeat and rout over the Chinese border and we were back again at the point at which British and Czech co-operation had arrived a year previously.

CHAPTER XXIV

GENERAL CONCLUSIONS

BEFORE we decide our policy as to withdrawal or otherwise from Russia it is necessary to know whether we have contracted any obligations to the Russian people, and what is the nature of such obligations, if any. Are they moral, military, or political?

Towards the end of 1914, when our army had been driven back behind the Marne and the future of Europe and our Empire was in the balance, frantic appeals were made by British statesmen, and even by still more august authority, asking Russia to rush to our aid and save us from destruction. This appeal was backed by British public and Labour opinion, and through our Press made a profound impression upon the Russian people. The Russian Government, regardless of their best military advice, forced their partially mobilised legions to make a rapid flying raid into East Prussia, which immediately reduced the pressure upon our own armies and made the victory of the Marne possible. Hurriedly mobilised, imperfectly equipped, not too brilliantly led, these legions, constituting the chivalry of Russia, became the prey of Prussia's perfect military machine. The Russian Government never dared to tell the Russian peasant the number of Russian souls who were mutilated by high explosives and smothered in the cold Masurian

General Conclusions

marshes in that sublime effort to save her friends. Russia lost as many men in saving Paris during that raid as did all the other Allies in the first year of the war.

Russia continued to fight and mobilise until 1917, by which time she had collected a huge army of over twelve million men. The Hohenzollern dynasty and its military advisers came to the conclusion that it would soon be impossible to stem this human tide by ordinary military means, and having a complete understanding of Russian psychology through its dynastic and administrative agents, decided to undermine the *moral* of the Russian people. German " Black Books " were not employed against British leaders exclusively. We need not wonder at the rapid spread among Russians of suspicion against their civil and military leaders when we remember that the same sort of propaganda admittedly influenced the administration of justice in England. The people of Russia were true to their friends, demoralisation and decomposition began at the head, rapidly filtering down to the lowest strata of society.

If the Allied cause was deserted, it was the desertion of a ruling class, not of a people or its army. German treachery wormed its way in at the top, and so destroyed a great race it never could have conquered.

Having disorganised the Russian military machine, Germany sent her agents to continue the disorder and prevent recovery. She secured the Brest-Litovsk Treaty, and made a levy of several hundred millions sterling upon her bailiffs, whom she put in possession of her neighbour's property. Lenin and Trotsky found anarchy the most effective weapon to further the interest of their masters and protect their Eastern flank. A peace which virtually extended German conquest to the hinterland of Tsing-Tchau was dangerous to every civilising influence in the Far East.

The Bolshevik treaty was not less dangerous to Europe herself, since it brought a war-like population of one hundred and eighty millions within the sphere of German military influence.

The British Expeditionary Force was ordered to Siberia in June, 1918, to assist the orderly elements of Russian society to reorganise themselves under a national Government and to resurrect and reconstruct the Russian front. Firstly, to enable Russia to resist German aggression; secondly, to weaken German military power on the Western front, where at that time she was again delivering hammer-blows at the gates of Paris. This expedition was approved by every party and patriot in Britain, and the only criticism offered at the time was that it should have been so long delayed. Soviet power under German and Austrian direction had released the German and Austrian prisoners of war, armed and organised them into formidable armies to perform the double task of maintaining their creatures in power at Moscow and extending their domination over a helpless friendly Allied Power.

There was every reason for treating the Dictatorship of Lenin and Trotsky as a mere side-show of the German military party; they were, in fact, a

General Conclusions

branch of the military problem with which the Allies were bound to deal. Under Entente direction anti-Bolshevik Governments were established, and were promised the unstinted help of the Allies to recover their territory and expel the agents of the enemy who had so foully polluted their own home. It was on this understanding that Admiral Koltchak, by herculean efforts, hurled the German hirelings over the Urals, and awaited near Vatka the advance of the Allies from Archangel preparatory to a march on Petrograd. Alas! he waited for seven long months in vain; the Allies never came! After expending his last ounce of energy and getting so near to final victory, we failed him at the post. Why?

The menace to our own armies in France had disappeared; there was, I suppose, no longer an urgent necessity to re-establish the Russian front, though the possibility of such re-establishment had kept huge German forces practically demobilised near the Russian and Ukrainian frontiers. Koltchak and his gallant comrade Denikin had served the Entente purpose. Lenin and Trotsky, by wholesale intimidation and murder, had aroused the enthusiasm of similarly disposed compatriots in Allied countries. These compatriots were becoming noisy in the constituencies. The establishment of order to enable the Russian people to establish a clean democratic Government, and arise from their nightmare of unbridled anarchy, while very desirable in itself, was not a good party cry in any of the Western democracies. I grant all these things; but what about honour? Has this no longer any place in the political curriculum of the Allied Powers?

These are only some of the things it is necessary to remember before we finally decide to desert a temporarily sick friend. If I were the ruler of a state I should pray the gods to preserve me from half-hearted Allies and over-cautious friends. If I wished to help a fallen state or lend an honest hand in a great cause, whether it were to eradicate a hideous and fatal national malady or assert a principle of right and justice, first shield me from the palsy of Allied diplomacy! One clear-sighted, honest helper is worth a dozen powerful aiders whose main business is to put obstacles in each other's way.

If we were discussing the question of Allied interference before the fact, I could give many reasons for remaining neutral; but we have to recognise that for their own purposes they have interfered, that their Military Missions and forces have been operating in the country for over a year, during which time they have made commitments and given pledges of a more or less binding character. That these commitments and pledges are not the irresponsible acts of subordinates on the spot, but have been made by Allied statesmen, both in and out of their several Parliaments; and in this respect our national leaders are no exception to the rule. Without filling my pages with quotations, readers will be able to find and tabulate such for themselves. So categorical are the nature of these that it is impossible to imagine them to have been made without fully understanding their import and sig-

General Conclusions

nificance to the orderly section of the Russian people who, on the faith of these pledges, gave us their trust.

It cannot, therefore, be a discussion upon interference or non-interference; *that* has long since been disposed of by our words and acts. It is now a question whether we shall withdraw from Russia because we have thought fit to change our attitude to the Russian problem. It is certain that our decision to-day upon this subject will decide our future relations with this great people. If you desert a friend in his hour of need, you cannot expect that he will be particularly anxious to help you when he has thrown off his ill-health and is in a position to give valuable help to those who gave succour in his distress.

If our desertion turns this people from us, they will become the prey of our recent enemies, and if that happens we can prate about the Treaty of Paris as much as we like. The Teuton will have more than balanced the account.

INDEX

271

Index

Index

273

Index

Index

275

Index

Index

Index

PRINTED BY CASSELL & COMPANY, LIMITED, LA BELLE SAUVAGE, LONDON, E.C.4
F 35.22Q

www.ingramcontent.com/pod-product-compliance
Lightning Source LLC
Chambersburg PA
CBHW030408100426
42812CB00028B/2877/J